T0343853

NEW
Close-up
English in Use

B1

Philip James

Additional material: Emma Fox

NATIONAL
GEOGRAPHIC
LEARNING

Australia • Brazil • Canada • Mexico • Singapore • United Kingdom • United States

Contents

Unit	Grammar	Vocabulary and Use of English
13 pages 81–86	question tags; subject and object questions; negative questions	sentence transformation; collocations and expressions; open cloze; multiple-cloze; speaking
14 pages 87–91	past perfect simple; past simple and past perfect simple; past perfect continuous	prepositions; open cloze; multiple-choice cloze; writing
15 pages 92–97	modals and semi-modals (1)	sentence transformation; word formation; multiple-choice cloze; open cloze; speaking
16 pages 98–102	modals and semi-modals (2)	phrasal verbs; open cloze; multiple-choice cloze; writing
Review 4 pages 103–106	Grammar Use of English: word formation; open cloze; Grammar and Vocabulary	
17 pages 107–111	the passive; *by* and *with*	prepositions; open cloze; multiple-choice cloze; speaking
18 pages 112–116	passive sentences with modals; the passive: other tenses	sentence transformation; collocations and expressions; open cloze; multiple-choice cloze; writing
19 pages 117–122	reported speech: statements; *say* and *tell*	phrasal verbs, open cloze; multiple-choice cloze; speaking
20 pages 123–128	reported speech: changes to pronouns, possessives, time and place; reported speech: questions	sentence transformation; word formation; open cloze; multiple-choice cloze; writing
Review 5 pages 129–132	Grammar Use of English: word formation; open cloze; Grammar and Vocabulary	
21 pages 133–137	the causative	sentence transformation; collocations and expressions; open cloze; multiple-choice cloze; speaking
22 pages 138–143	*-ing* form; *to* + infinitive; infinitives (without *to*); *-ing* form or *to* + infinitive?	prepositions; word formation; open cloze; multiple-choice cloze; writing
23 pages 144–148	ordering adjectives; adjectives ending in *-ed* and *-ing*; types of adverbs; order of adverbs (manner, place and time); order of adverbs (degree and frequency); *so* and *such*	phrasal verbs; word formation; open cloze; multiple-choice cloze; speaking
24 pages 149–153	*comparison of adjectives and adverbs; other comparative structures*	sentence transformation; word formation; open cloze; multiple-choice cloze; writing
Review 6 pages 154–157	Grammar Use of English: open cloze; word formation; Grammar and Vocabulary	

1 Which of these sentences are correct (C) and incorrect (I)?

1 Mum's plane arrives at 10.15. _C_
2 My grandad is always saying I'm funny. _C_
3 Oh no! It snows heavily at the moment. _I_
4 She's thinking about going home for the holidays. _C_
5 You're seeming angry. Did I do something? _I_

6 Are you believing what I say? _I_
7 Kevin likes visiting his cousins in Scotland. _C_
8 My older sisters live in the city centre. _C_
9 I'm not understanding why you argue with your sister. _I_
10 What do you think about right now? _I_

How many did you get right? ☐

Grammar

Present simple

Affirmative	Negative	Questions
I / We / You / They walk. He / She / It walk**s**.	I / We / You / They **don't** walk. He / She / It **doesn't** walk.	**Do** I / we / you / they walk? **Does** he / she / it walk?
Short answers		
Yes, I / we / you / they **do**. **Yes**, he / she / it **does**.	**No**, I / we / you / they **don't**. **No**, he / she / it **doesn't**.	

We use the present simple for:

- scientific facts or general truths.
  *The sun **rises** in the east.*
- habits or routines (often with adverbs of frequency).
  *He often **watches** TV in the evenings.*
- permanent situations.
  *She **works** in the city centre.*
- timetabled or scheduled events in the future.
  *My lessons **start** at nine o'clock in the morning.*

> **Note**
>
> We often use these common time expressions with the present simple: *every day / week / month / summer, every other day, once a week, twice a month, at the weekend, in January, in the morning / afternoon / evening, at night, on Tuesdays, on Friday mornings, etc.*
> *I get up at seven o'clock **every morning**.*

Adverbs of frequency

We use adverbs of frequency to say how often something happens. They come before the main verb, but after the verb *be*.
*Sheila **is always** busy at the weekends.*
*Jason **hardly ever eats** out at restaurants.*

Some common adverbs of frequency are:
always (most often), *usually, often, sometimes, rarely / hardly ever / seldom, never* (least often).

Present continuous

Affirmative	Negative	Quetions
I **am** (**'m**) walk**ing**. He / She / It **is** (**'s**) walk**ing**. We / You / They **are** (**'re**) walk**ing**.	I **am** (**'m**) **not** walk**ing**. He / She / It **is not** (**isn't**) walk**ing**. We / You / They **are not** (**aren't**) walk**ing**.	**Am** I walk**ing**? **Is** he / she / it walk**ing**? **Are** we / you / they walk**ing**?
Short answers		
Yes, I **am**. **Yes**, he / she / it **is**. **Yes**, we / you / they **are**.	**No**, I'm **not**. **No**, he / she / it **isn't**. **No**, we / you / they **aren't**.	

Spelling: take → tak**ing**, get → ge**tting**, fly → fly**ing**

We use the present continuous for:
- actions that are in progress at or around the time of speaking.

*My parents **are travelling** for work right now.*

- actions or situations that are temporary.

*I'**m doing** a course at work this week.*

- situations that are changing or developing in the present.

*More and more people **are losing** their jobs.*

- annoying habits (often with *always, continually, constantly* and *forever*).

*My brother **is** continually **telling** me to clean my bedroom.*

- plans and arrangements for the future.

*We'**re having** a family get-together on Saturday evening.*

Note

We use these common time expressions with the present continuous: *at the moment, now, for the time being, this morning / afternoon / evening / week / month / year, today,* etc. *My younger sister is staying with me **for the time being***.

Stative verbs

Some verbs are not usually used in continuous tenses. They are called *stative* because they describe states and not actions. To talk about the present, we use these verbs in the present simple tense. The most common of these are:

- verbs of emotion: *hate, like, love, need, prefer, want.*

*Peter **hates** his new job.*

- verbs of senses: *feel, hear, see, smell, sound, taste.*

*These flowers **smell** wonderful.*

- verbs which express a state of mind: *believe, doubt, forget, imagine, know, remember, seem, suppose, think, understand.*

*I **doubt** Mum will be home in time for dinner.*

- verbs of possession: *belong to, have, own, possess.*

*Do you know who **owns** that blue car in the street?*

- other verbs: *be, consist, contain, cost, include, mean.*

*The price **includes** flights and accommodation.*

Some verbs can be both stative verbs and action verbs, but with a different meaning. These are the most common.

be	*Pat **is** very reliable.* (usual behaviour)
	*Toby **is being** naughty.* (at the moment; not his normal behaviour)
expect	*I **expect** Mum will go to the shops on her way home.* (expect = think or believe)
	*We'**re expecting** an email from my older sister.* (expect = wait for)
have	*Penny **has** a huge garden.* (= own / possess)
	*Trent **is having** a great time on holiday.* (= experience)
	*Brad **is having** a working lunch today.* (= eating)
taste	*This sauce **tastes** awful!* (= have a particular flavour)
	*Why **are you tasting** the soup?* (= test the flavour)
think	*I **think** that actor is very funny.* (= have an opinion)
	*Janet **is thinking** of studying politics at university.* (= consider)
see	*'My aunt Sue is my dad's sister.' 'Oh, I **see**.'* (understand)
	*I'**m seeing** my college friends later today.* (= meet)
smell	*This soap **smells** like roses.* (= have a particular smell)
	*Why **are you smelling** the milk?* (= action of smelling)
weigh	*Pete **weighs** 53 kilograms.* (= have a particular weight)
	*I'**m weighing** the flour and sugar for the cake.* (= measure the weight)

1

Grammar exercises

2 **Choose the correct option (a–b) to complete the sentences.**

1 Get up, William! Why ___ so lazy this morning?
    a are you be   **(b)** are you being

2 Who's that? I ___ her name.
    a 'm not remembering   **(b)** don't remember

3 Irene ___ a house with her friends for the time being.
    a share   **(b)** is sharing

4 Grandad isn't feeling well. He ___ the doctor later today.
    (a) 's seeing   **b** sees

5 Penny ___ of becoming a firefighter.
    (a) is thinking   **b** thinks

6 Sam ___ his sister.
    a is looking like   **(b)** looks like

7 Mum and Dad always ___ us on holiday with them.
    (a) take   **b** are taking

8 The cook ___ the sauce at the moment to see if it's too salty.
    a tastes   **(b)** is tasting

9 Tomas and Julia ___ to their aunt's house every weekend.
    a are going   **(b)** go

10 Why ___ so many young people are out of work?
    (a) do you think   **b** are you thinking

3 **Complete the sentences with the present simple or present continuous form of the verbs.**

1 Katia ___*is finding*___ (find) it difficult to make friends in her new job. She ___*doesn't seem*___ (not / seem) to be able to talk to people easily.

2 Look! It ___*'s raining*___ (rain). It ___*rarely rains*___ (rarely / rain) in Greece in the summer.

3 Joe ___*is seeing*___ (see) the dentist tomorrow.

4 She ___*'s riding*___ (ride) her bike at the moment. She ___*rides*___ (ride) her bike every evening before she ___*has*___ (have) dinner.

5 Mum ___*gets*___ (get) a call from my brother twice a week. He ___*'s travelling*___ (travel) round the USA for six months and ___*never forgets*___ (never / forget) to phone her.

6 When I ___*do*___ (do) something kind for my family, I ___*feel*___ (feel) great!

7 Marek can't come out to play because he ___*'s doing*___ (do) his homework. He ___*does*___ (do) his homework every afternoon at this time.

8 *Do they always phone* (they / always / phone) your grandparents before they go to visit?

4 Match the questions (1–10) with their answers (a–j).

1 Do your grandparents live near you? | *h* | **a** An apple.
2 Where are you going on holiday this summer? | *j* | **b** No, I'm not.
3 Do I seem confident when I'm in class? | *c* | **c** Yes, you do.
4 Is it cold out today? | *e* | **d** No, she isn't.
5 Are the children doing their homework? | *g* | **e** Yes, it is.
6 What's your brother eating now? | *a* | **f** Every six weeks.
7 Is your aunt an architect? | *d* | **g** Yes, they are.
8 Does your nephew work full-time? | *i* | **h** No, they don't.
9 How often do you go to your hairdresser? | *f* | **i** Yes, he does.
10 Are you going to the cinema with your parents tonight? | *b* | **j** To Canada.

5 Complete the sentences with the present simple or present continuous form of the verbs.

1 **a** My sister ___*is*___ (be) a serious, honest and hard-working person.
b Why ___*are you being*___ (you / be) so unkind to your brother today?
2 **a** He ___*'s seeing*___ (see) the doctor later this week.
b Do you ___*see*___ (see) what I mean now?
3 **a** How much ___*does your dad weigh*___ (your dad / weigh)?
b The cook ___*is weighing*___ (weigh) the meat now – he needs a kilo.
4 **a** I ___*expect*___ (expect) she's very nervous about the exam.
b She ___*'s expecting*___ (expect) a letter from her grandma in the post today.
5 **a** Your cousins ___*have*___ (have) a really nice home.
b What time ___*are you having*___ (you / have) lunch with Tom today?
6 **a** I ___*'m thinking*___ (think) of going to South America next summer.
b I ___*think*___ (think) her new book is fantastic.

6 Use the prompts to write questions.

1 you / eat / with your parents / every evening?
Do you eat with your parents every evening?
2 what time / your dad / usually / get home from work?
What time does your dad usually get home from work?
3 how many languages / your niece / speak?
How many languages does your niece speak?
4 you / wash / your hair at the moment?
Are you washing your hair at the moment?
5 why / you / smell / the fish?
Why are you smelling the fish?
6 who / you / usually / walk / to school with?
Who do you usually walk to school with?
7 she / think / go / to university?
Is she thinking of going to university?
8 whose / car / you / wash / now?
Whose car are you washing now?

1

Sentence transformation

7 Complete the second sentence so that it has a similar meaning to the first sentence, using the word given. Do not change the word given. You must use between two and five words.

1 I have an appointment to see the hairdresser on Monday.
I _____*'m / am seeing*_____ the hairdresser on Monday. **AM**

2 They seldom go anywhere without their children.
They _____*don't / do not often go*_____ anywhere without their children. **OFTEN**

3 I don't think that expensive bike belongs to him.
I doubt _____*he owns*_____ that expensive bike. **OWNS**

4 Kat resembles Rebecca because they're sisters.
Kat _____*looks like*_____ Rebecca because they're sisters. **LIKE**

5 My mum complains about my messy bedroom all the time.
My mum _____*is forever complaining*_____ about my messy bedroom. **FOREVER**

6 Fran nearly always does her homework before she has dinner.
Fran _____*hardly ever does her homework*_____ after dinner. **HARDLY**

7 My baby brother is very light!
My baby brother _____*doesn't / does not weigh*_____ very much! **WEIGH**

8 The temperature is dropping every day; winter is coming.
It _____*'s / is getting colder*_____ every day; winter is coming. **GETTING**

Vocabulary

Collocations and expressions

8 Complete the sentences with these verbs.

| apply | design | get (x2) | give | go | make | travel | wait | work |

1 Can you _give_ me some advice?
2 He needs to _work_ on a project.
3 Please don't _get_ annoyed with me.
4 I never _wait_ a long time for a bus.
5 Why don't you _apply_ for that job?

6 Do you want to _get_ married?
7 It's amazing we can _travel_ into space.
8 I'm bored. Let's _make_ a video.
9 Architects _design_ buildings.
10 Dan wants to _go_ to university.

Word formation

9 Use the word in capitals to form a word that fits in the gap.

1 You don't need to study at university to get good _qualifications_ . **QUALIFY**
2 My uncle isn't working at the moment – he's _unemployed_ . **EMPLOY**
3 I love books, so I want to become a _librarian_ . **LIBRARY**
4 She works as a camera _operator_ on different film sets. **OPERATION**
5 Why are you looking so _miserable_ ? What's the matter? **MISERY**
6 Why does he want to work at the holiday camp? He isn't very _sociable_ . **SOCIAL**
7 He's training to become a _lawyer_ at the moment. **LAW**
8 Candidates for the job need to be very _reliable_ . **RELY**
9 Sometimes it's difficult to believe what _politicians_ say. **POLITICS**
10 You're very _cheerful_ ! Is it because the sun is shining? **CHEER**

Exam practice

Open cloze

10 For each question, write the correct answer. Write one word for each gap.

1 My mum ___*does*___ not work in an office. She works on a farm.
2 The children ___*always*___ do their homework on Fridays – they never do it at the weekend.
3 Why aren't you ___*wearing*___ your seat belt? Please put it on!
4 He rarely ___*travels*___ for work, but right now he's in the USA.
5 We're ___*having*___ breakfast at the moment. Can I call you later?
6 I'm ___*going*___ to a job fair at the weekend. Do you want to come?
7 My nephew is ___*thinking*___ of joining the Spanish club at school.
8 Who does that big black car ___*belong*___ to?

Multiple-choice cloze

11 For each question, choose the correct answer.

1 The ___ are training hard for the 100-metre race.
   A architects　　　B astronauts　　　**(C)** athletes　　　D accountants

2 Soldiers are often in very ___ situations.
   A calm　　　**(B)** dangerous　　　C anxious　　　D nervous

3 Our sister hates parties – she's always so ___ around people.
   A honest　　　**(B)** shy　　　C jealous　　　D relaxed

4 I love the theatre – I want to be ___ .
   A an engineer　　　**(B)** an actor　　　C a nurse　　　D a lawyer

5 Peter isn't a great teacher. He isn't very ___ .
   (A) patient　　　B lazy　　　C generous　　　D jealous

6 We don't like the new building in town. It's really ___ .
   A serious　　　B unkind　　　C lazy　　　**(D)** ugly

7 My grandad doesn't work anymore – he's ___ .
   (A) retired　　　B strong　　　C fit　　　D careful

8 She's from a large ___ . She's got five brothers!
   A home　　　B house　　　C place　　　**(D)** family

Speaking

12 Work in pairs. Discuss the questions.

- How many people are there in your family?
- What do you usually do with your family at the weekend?
- Are you doing anything fun with your parents this weekend? What?
- Describe a typical weekday.
- Where do your parents / members of your family work?
- What jobs do you think are interesting?

Unit 2

1 **Which of these sentences are correct (C) and incorrect (I)?**

1 Did Sam do any homework at the weekend? C
2 There isn't much food in the house. C
3 My parents works for the same company. I
4 Maths is very difficult for some students. C
5 Is there some plastic boxes in the bin? I

6 I've got three cousins – Tony, Joe and Sue. C
7 Can I borrow some money from you, please? C
8 Are there some chocolate in the fridge? I
9 Salt aren't good for your health. I
10 There is a wooden bowl on the table. C

How many did you get right? ☐

Grammar

Countable nouns

Most nouns are countable and have singular and plural forms.

sister → sisters   toy → toys   leaf → leaves   woman → women
family → families   tomato → tomatoes   child → children   foot → feet

We usually use *a* or *an* with singular countable nouns.
a cook
an idea

We can use *some, any* or a number (e.g. *two*) with plural countable nouns.
*There are **some** flowers in the field.*
*Are there **any** potatoes?*
*I'm leaving my job in **two** weeks.*

We use singular or plural verb forms with countable nouns depending on whether we are talking about one item or more.
*A weekend away **is** just what they need.*
*My nephews **live** in Manchester.*

> **Note**
> Some countable nouns don't end in -s.
> Remember to use a plural verb form with them.
> *Children **are** sometimes very noisy!*
> *His feet **are** growing.*

Uncountable nouns

Some nouns are uncountable. They do not have plural forms.

advice	food	history	luggage	progress	time
cheese	fruit	homework	milk	research	traffic
chocolate	fun	information	money	rubbish	water
equipment	furniture	knowledge	music	salt	weather

We don't use *a* or *an* with uncountable nouns. We can use *some* and *any*.
*I'd like **some** water, please.*
*Is there **any** sport on TV tonight?*

We always use singular verb forms with uncountable nouns.
*This cheese **is** very tasty.*
*Juice **isn't** good for your teeth.*

We can use phrases describing quantity with uncountable nouns to say how much we have.
The most common of these phrases are:

a bag of	a cup of	a number of
a bottle of	a glass of	a packet of
a bowl of	a jar of	a piece of
a can of	a kilo of	a tin of
a carton of	a loaf of	

*I'll prepare **a bowl of** fruit.*   *Would you like **a cup of** tea?*

> **Note**
> Some uncountable nouns end in -s.
> Remember to use a singular verb form with them.
> *The news **is** very good!*
> *Physics **isn't** an easy subject.*

Quantifiers

We use *some* with both uncountable and plural countable nouns in affirmative sentences and in requests or offers.
*Here are **some magazines** for you to read.*
*Can you send me **some information**, please?*
*Would you like **some cheese** in your sandwich?*

We use *any* with both uncountable and plural countable nouns in negative sentences and in questions.
*Billy hasn't got **any sisters**.*
*Did Mum buy **any chocolate** at the shops?*

We use *a lot / lots of* with both uncountable and plural countable nouns.
*I've got lots **of luggage** to take on my trip.*
*There are **a lot of people** in this city.*

We use *a little* with uncountable nouns and *a few* with plural countable nouns in affirmative sentences.
*I like **a little sugar** in my coffee.*
*Kevin always has **a few sandwiches** for lunch.*

We use *much* with uncountable nouns and *many* with plural countable nouns in negative sentences and in questions.
*There wasn't **much rain** last year.*
*Have you got **many friends**, Steve?*

Grammar exercises

2 Write countable (C) or uncountable (U).

1	brother	C	**6** family	C	**11** toy	C
2	woman	C	**7** equipment	U	**12** news	U
3	traffic	U	**8** foot	C	**13** knowledge	U
4	weather	U	**9** furniture	U	**14** maths	U
5	tomato	C	**10** research	U	**15** child	C

3 Complete with *a*, *an* or *some*.

1 I want to be ¹ _____an_____ architect when I'm older.

2 **A:** What's that, Mum?
   B: It's ² _____an_____ old necklace that Grandma gave me.

3 I saw ³ _____some_____ cool computer equipment and ⁴ _____an_____ amazing video game in a shop this morning.

4 **A:** The cook wants to make ⁵ _____an_____ apple cake, but there are only two apples.
   B: I'll go and buy ⁶ _____some_____ .

5 **A:** What do you want for your birthday?
   B: I want ⁷ _____a_____ book about music and ⁸ _____some_____ delicious chocolate!

6 **A:** Could I have ⁹ _____some_____ milk?
   B: Oh, sorry, there isn't ¹⁰ _____any_____ left.

7 **A:** Did you buy ¹¹ _____a_____ gift for your aunt?
   B: Yes, I bought her ¹² _____an_____ Italian handbag.

8 Do you want ¹³ _____some_____ sugar in your coffee?

9 I need ¹⁴ _____a_____ loaf of bread and ¹⁵ _____a_____ carton of juice.

10 **A:** Would you like ¹⁶ _____some_____ fruit, Maria?
   B: Yes, please. I'd like ¹⁷ _____an_____ orange and ¹⁸ _____some_____ grapes.

4 Choose the correct option to complete the sentences.

1 How many children *was* / *were* there at your sister's party?
2 Some people never *get* / *gets* a good job.
3 There *is* / *are* a kilo of sugar in the cupboard.
4 Maths *is* / *are* Jody's favourite subject at school.
5 Where *is* / *are* the baby's toys?
6 The music *is* / *are* too loud!
7 The women at my office *is* / *are* really sociable.
8 The advice you're giving me *is* / *are* very helpful.
9 I'm afraid the news about your exam *isn't* / *aren't* good.
10 My parents *is* / *are* visiting friends at the moment.

5 Complete the conversation with *some* or *any*.

Julie: I don't know what to pack for this holiday camp! Mum – I need ¹ ___some___ advice!

Mum: OK, Julie. Let's make a list. First, you need ² ___some___ comfortable clothes. Take ³ ___some___ sun cream, too.

Julie: Oh, I haven't got ⁴ ___any___ . I need to buy a bottle.

Mum: What about at night if it's cold? Do you need to take ⁵ ___any___ blankets?

Julie: Good idea. And ⁶ ___some___ matches for a camp fire!

Mum: Mmm, I don't want you to take ⁷ ___any___ matches. I'm sure the camp leaders have got ⁸ ___some___ boxes of matches.

Julie: Right. Is there ⁹ ___any___ equipment I need?

Mum: What about your compass? And a radio so you can listen to ¹⁰ ___some___ music?

Julie: OK! And what about snacks? I've got a big bar of chocolate, but I haven't got ¹¹ ___any___ packets of crisps.

Mum: You also need a water bottle. And don't forget to take your toothbrush and ¹² ___some___ money!

Julie: Great. Thanks, Mum!

6 Tick the correct sentences. Then correct the mistakes.

1 There are a large number of people at my brother's office.
   There is a large number of people at my brother's office.

2 In Japan, womans often wear white kimonos on their wedding day.
   In Japan, women often wear white kimonos on their wedding day.

3 Young children is often upset when their parents raise their voices.
   Young children are often upset when their parents raise their voices.

4 My family history is very interesting.
   ✓

5 Do you know what the weather is like in Argentina in January?
   ✓

6 Are there a lot of traffic when you drive to work?
   Is there a lot of traffic when you drive to work?

7 Sara, can you buy a loaf of water on your way home?
   Sara, can you buy a loaf of bread / bottle of water on your way home?

8 My sister is applying for lots of jobs right now.
   ✓

Sentence transformation

7 Complete the second sentence so that it has a similar meaning to the first sentence, using the word given. Do not change the word given. You must use between two and five words.

1 These streets are too dangerous at night.
There _____*'s / is too much danger*_____ on these streets at night.   **TOO**

2 Shall I put sugar in your coffee?
Would you _____*like some sugar*_____ in your coffee?   **SOME**

3 Can you tell me the number of people who are going to college this year?
Can you tell me _____*how many people are*_____ going to college this year?   **HOW**

4 Dan and Helen haven't got much furniture for their new house.
Dan and Helen have only got _____*a few pieces of furniture*_____ for their new house.   **PIECES**

5 Dad hasn't got much time to cook dinner today.
Dad has only got _____*a little time*_____ to cook dinner today.   **A**

6 There are only three biscuits left in the bag.
There _____*aren't / are not many*_____ biscuits left in the bag.   **MANY**

7 Pablo has got many different qualifications.
Pablo has got _____*a lot of*_____ different qualifications.   **LOT**

8 Do you now if this café serves different kinds of vegetarian dishes?
Do you know if _____*there are any*_____ different vegetarian dishes on the menu in this café?   **ANY**

Vocabulary

Prepositions

8 Choose the correct prepositions.

1 be brought up *by* / *for* someone
2 get married *in* / *into*
3 go out *to* / *with* someone
4 split up *for* / *with* someone
5 wait a long time *by* / *for* something

6 run out *in* / *into* something
7 fight *to* / *for* something
8 due *about* / *to* something
9 be in trouble *at* / *with* someone
10 work *at* / *with* someone

9 Complete the sentences with the correct form of the prepositional phrases from Exercise 8.

1 We're hoping to _____*get married in*_____ my parent's garden. We haven't got many guests.
2 Please close the gate so the dog doesn't _____*run out into*_____ the road.
3 My cousin _____*is in trouble with*_____ my aunt because she isn't doing her homework.
4 I think it's important to _____*fight for*_____ the things you really believe in.
5 The children don't like to _____*wait a long time for*_____ their dinner!
6 Our friends will be late _____*due to*_____ the bad traffic.
7 My grandma _____*was brought up by*_____ her oldest sister.
8 My brother is really upset at the moment – his girlfriend says she wants to _____*split up with*_____ him.
9 He _____*works with*_____ a lot of lawyers and politicians.
10 I don't want to _____*go out with*_____ anyone. I just like being with my friends!

2

Exam practice

Open cloze

10 For each question, write the correct answer. Write one word for each gap.

1 Were there ___*many*___ people at your birthday party?

2 I've only got a ___*few*___ friends, but they're all kind and generous.

3 We would like some ___*information*___ about the job fair, please.

4 They need to make ___*an*___ appointment to see the hairdresser.

5 We need ___*a*___ lot of chocolate to make this cake.

6 Some pedestrians aren't very careful when they ___*cross*___ busy roads.

7 The firefighters are confident that they can put ___*out*___ the fire.

8 He only gets a small salary, so he's careful and doesn't spend ___*much*___ money.

Multiple-choice cloze

11 For each question, choose the correct answer.

1 Here are ___ books for you to borrow, Jack.
   A a little   B much   **C some**   D a

2 Can you help me do ___ research for my project, Dad?
   A much   B any   C a few   **D some**

3 Does your cousin have ___ part-time work?
   A lots   B a few   **C any**   D a lot

4 Would you like ___ tea, Bella?
   A lot of   **B some**   C a few   D many

5 Many young people haven't got ___ knowledge of old family traditions.
   A any   B many   C a lot   D a few

6 The waiter is serving ___ food today – the restaurant is very busy.
   A any   B much   **C lots of**   D a lot

7 There are ___ of families travelling during the month of August.
   A a lot   B a little   C a few   D much

8 The actor likes ___ time to relax before he goes onto the film set.
   A a few   **B a little**   C many   D much

9 Let's take a look at ___ different career options.
   A a few   B much   C a lot   D a little

10 How ___ of you want to travel into space?
   A much   B some   C any   **D many**

Writing

12 Read the writing task and write your answer in about 100 words. Try to use colloquial language, contractions and short sentences.

You receive an email from your friend who asks you about your family members and the jobs they do. Write an email to your friend giving information about your family members and their jobs. Say which job you prefer and why.

Unit 3

1 **Which of these sentences are correct (C) and incorrect (I)?**

1 Paul was eating all the biscuits this morning – there aren't any left!   _I_
2 Alia was making a dessert at two o'clock yesterday afternoon.   _C_
3 They wasn't having a snack when I arrived.   _I_
4 Tom never ate meat when he was younger.   _C_
5 We weren't going out to a restaurant last week.   _I_

6 The rain was falling and the children were looking at it miserably from the window.   _C_
7 Jamie and I tidyed the kitchen earlier today.   _I_
8 Did your uncle made an apple cake yesterday?   _I_
9 Dad prepared the potatoes and fried them an hour ago.   _C_
10 Were they eating lunch when you called?   _C_

How many did you get right? ☐

Grammar

Past simple

Affirmative	Negative	Questions
I / He / She / It / We / You / They cook**ed**.	I / He / She / It / We / You / They **didn't** cook.	**Did** I / he / she / it / we / you / they cook?
Short Answers		
Yes, I / he / she / it **did**. **Yes**, we / you / they **did**.	**No**, I / he / she / it **didn't**. **No**, we / you / they **didn't**.	

Spelling: dance → danc**ed**, travel → trave**lled**, ti**dy** → ti**died**, play → play**ed**

We use the past simple for:
- something that started and finished in the past.
*Mum **made** some sandwiches an hour ago.*
- past routines and habits (often with adverbs of frequency).
*Petra always **ate** lunch with her friends.*
- actions that happened one after the other in the past, for example when telling a story.
*The family **went** home and **had** a tasty dinner.*

> **Note**
> Some verbs are irregular and do not follow these spelling rules. See a list of irregular verbs on pages 158–159.

> **Note**
> We often use these common time expressions with the past simple: *yesterday, last night / week / month / summer, a week / month / year ago, twice a week, once a month, at the weekend, in March, in the morning / afternoon / evening, at night, on Thursdays, on Monday mornings*, etc.
> *The farmer planted some apple trees **last month**.*

Past continuous

Affirmative	Negative	Questions
I / He / She / It **was** cook**ing**. We / You / They **were** cook**ing**.	I / He / She / It **was not** (**wasn't**) cook**ing**. We / You / They **were not** (**weren't**) cook**ing**.	**Was** I / he / she / it cook**ing**? **Were** we / you / they cook**ing**?
Short Answers		
Yes, I / he / she / it was. Yes, we / you / they were.	No, I / he / she / it wasn't. No, we / you / they weren't.	

Spelling: dance → danc**ing**, travel → trave**lling**, ti**dy** → ti**dying**

We use the past continuous for:
- actions that were in progress at a specific time in the past.
*Dad **was cooking dinner** at six o'clock last night.*
- two or more actions that were in progress at the same time in the past.
*I **was doing** my homework while my sister **was playing** video games.*
- giving background information in a story.
*The sun **was shining** and the birds **were singing** in the trees.*
- an action that was in progress in the past that was interrupted by another action.
*We **were dancing** when the music stopped suddenly.*

Note

We often use these common time expressions with the past continuous: *while, as, all day / week / month / year, at ten o'clock last night, last Sunday / week / year, this morning,* etc.
*The engineers were working on the project **all month**.*

Grammar exercises

2 **Choose the correct option to complete the sentences.**

1 Billy was having / *was haveing* a snack at twelve o'clock last night.
2 *Were they going* / Did they go to the park for a picnic last weekend?
3 Was Susana frying / *Did Susana fry* onions a few minutes ago?
4 My grandma usually *was baking* / baked bread twice a week.
5 Dad was barbecuing the burgers while we were making / *make* a salad.
6 I *took* / was taking the cake out of the oven when I burned my hand.
7 We came home, went into the kitchen and *was boiling* / boiled water for tea.
8 Pam wasn't doing / *didn't do* the washing-up when I arrived.
9 Kieron broke / *was breaking* the water jug this morning.
10 My mum weren't *making* / didn't make lunch today.

3 **Complete the sentences with the past simple or past continuous form of the verbs.**

1 The farmer _____ was watering _____ (water) the tomatoes while his helper was planting some carrots.
2 Stefan _____ wasn't preparing _____ (not / prepare) vegetables when he cut his finger.
3 _____ Did they eat _____ (they / eat) at an expensive restaurant last Tuesday?
4 My father always _____ took _____ (take) his lunch to school when he was a boy.
5 _____ Were you making _____ (you / make) dinner when cooker broke?
6 The cook fried the eggs, _____ added _____ (add) some salt and served the meal.
7 My sister _____ didn't bake _____ (not / bake) the cake two hours ago; it's still hot.
8 The moon and the stars _____ were shining _____ (shine) in the night sky and everyone was sleeping.

4 Tick the correct sentences. Then correct the mistakes.

1 She was making pasta and meatballs for dinner last night.
  She made pasta and meatballs for dinner last night.

2 Did they serve vegetarian dishes at the café?
  ✓

3 My parents weren't having time for breakfast this morning.
  My parents didn't have time for breakfast this morning.

4 Did Peter take a cooking course last month?
  ✓

5 I was believing her when she said she wanted to pay for my meal.
  I believed her when she said she wanted to pay for my meal.

6 I was really hungry, but Cleo wasn't.
  ✓

7 While we were shopping at the food market, my brother was losing his backpack.
  While we were shopping at the food market, my brother lost his backpack.

8 We didn't eat our lunch when Siya arrived.
  We weren't eating our lunch when Siya arrived.

5 Find the mistake and write A or B in the box. Then correct the mistakes.

1 Gia was talking (A) on the phone when her dinner was starting (B) to burn. [B]
  Gia was talking on the phone when her dinner started to burn.

2 Jon was researching online when (A) his dad was working (B) in the garden. [A]
  Jon was researching online while his dad was working in the garden.

3 Penny was opening (A) the cupboard and found (B) a bar of chocolate. [A]
  Penny opened the cupboard and found a bar of chocolate.

4 While we were (A) on holiday, we were eating (B) in restaurants every evening. [B]
  While we were on holiday, we ate in restaurants every evening.

5 At eight o'clock last night, my sister was making (A) pancakes while I studied (B). [B]
  At eight o'clock last night, my sister was making pancakes while I was studying.

6 While Marek was working (A) in the garden, Jakob was arriving (B). [B]
  While Marek was working in the garden, Jakob arrived.

6 Write questions with the past simple or past continuous form. Then complete the short answers.

1 we / have coffee / at the café / twice last week
  A: *Did we have coffee at the café twice last week?*   B: No, ___*we didn't*___.

2 your parents / work / while / you sleep
  A: *Were you parents working while you were sleeping?*   B: No, ___*they weren't*___.

3 he / do a cooking course / when / he live in France
  A: *Did he do a cooking course when he lived in France?*   B: Yes, ___*he did*___.

4 your aunt / always / bake cakes / when / she be younger
  A: *Did your aunt always bake cakes when she was younger?*   B: No, ___*she didn't*___.

5 Sienna and Jake / eat at the diner / at 8 p.m. last night
  A: *Were Sienna and Jake eating at the diner at 8 p.m. last night?*   B: Yes, ___*they were*___.

6 Alex / follow a healthy eating plan / last month
  A: *Did Alex follow a healthy eating plan last month?*   B: No, ___*he didn't*___.

3

Sentence transformation

7 Complete the second sentence so that it has a similar meaning to the first sentence, using the word given. Do not change the word given. You must use between two and five words.

1 I prepared breakfast. At the same time, my sister made coffee.
   My sister was making coffee _____ *while I was preparing* _____ breakfast.   **WHILE**

2 Stella and Milo started baking biscuits at nine o'clock and they finished at ten o'clock.
   Stella and Milo _____ *were baking* _____ biscuits from nine o'clock to ten o'clock.   **BAKING**

3 I rarely ate my school lunch.
   I _____ *did not eat* _____ my school lunch very often.   **NOT**

4 We arrived for dinner. Sara was asleep.
   Sara _____ *was sleeping when* _____ we arrived for dinner.   **SLEEPING**

5 Karl was in the bath. He dropped his phone in the water.
   Karl _____ *was having a bath when* _____ he dropped his phone the water.   **HAVING**

6 My uncle left the office at six o'clock. It's now eight o'clock.
   Two _____ *hours ago* _____ , my uncle left the office.   **AGO**

7 I worked on Saturday and Sunday, unfortunately.
   I was _____ *working all weekend* _____ , unfortunately.   **WEEKEND**

8 She didn't feel safe while she was walking home last night.
   She _____ *felt unsafe* _____ while she was walking home last night.   **UNSAFE**

Vocabulary

Phrasal verbs

8 Complete the sentences with the correct form of these verbs.

| come (x2)   cut   eat   find   get   go   look (x2)   take |

1 How can we _____ *find* _____ out which restaurants are good for families?
2 Next, I _____ *cut* _____ up all the vegetables.
3 Do you like _____ *eating* _____ out at the weekend?
4 When the cake _____ *came* _____ out of the oven, it was completely burned!
5 I need to _____ *look* _____ up the answer.

6 Is the new café easy to _____ *get* _____ to?
7 Could you _____ *take* _____ the milk out of the fridge, please?
8 Please _____ *come* _____ back again soon.
9 They _____ *went* _____ out on Friday night.
10 If you're in Spain, _____ *look* _____ out for the traditional stews.

Word formation

9 Use the word in the capitals to form a word that fits in the gap.

1 Would you like still or _____ *sparkling* _____ water?   **SPARKLE**
2 The café has a very _____ *relaxed* _____ feel – it's a great place to read a book.   **RELAX**
3 The three-course lunch was _____ *absolutely* _____ delicious!   **ABSOLUTE**
4 If you want tasty food which is _____ *inexpensive* _____ , try the local Italian restaurant.   **EXPENSIVE**
5 I try to avoid giving the children _____ *processed* _____ food like burgers.   **PROCESS**
6 This pasta is completely _____ *tasteless* _____ – it needs some salt!   **TASTE**
7 He looked in the cupboard for some _____ *packets* _____ of rice, but there weren't any.   **PACK**
8 Have you got any _____ *recommendations* _____ for Chinese restaurants?   **RECOMMEND**
9 This is a lovely salad. It looks very _____ *colourful* _____ .   **COLOUR**
10 Not all curries are _____ *spicy* _____ , but they're always full of flavour.   **SPICE**

Exam practice

Open cloze

10 For each question, write the correct answer. Write one word for each gap.

1 The students ___were___ eating snacks in class this morning and they got into trouble.
2 ___Was___ he sitting in the café when you saw him?
3 We ___did___ not have breakfast at eight o'clock this morning; we had it at nine o'clock.
4 ___Were___ you baking bread all morning?
5 My cousin was preparing potatoes ___while___ I was frying onions.
6 I wasn't working at two o'clock yesterday afternoon; I was ___having___ a late lunch.
7 Mark was planting flowers in the garden ___when___ it started raining.
8 ___Did___ you go to the new French restaurant last week?

Multiple-choice cloze

11 For each question, choose the correct answer.

1 The doctor recommended a ___ eating plan and more exercise.
  A quick   B light   C fast   **D** healthy

2 We went to an American diner for my birthday. It was like ___ back in time to the 1950s!
  A going   B coming   C taking   D getting

3 I'm trying to reduce food ___ by making soup from old vegetables I find in my fridge.
  A size   **B** waste   C bill   D bags

4 Thanks for cooking me dinner – it ___ delicious! What is it?
  A looks   B sees   C sounds   D watches

5 The chef ___ the record for making the biggest pizza in the city.
  A cut   **B** broke   C served   D did

6 They were eating in ___ restaurants every week, which was really bad for them.
  A fast-food   B traditional   C modern   D old-fashioned

7 We only go out to expensive restaurants for very ___ occasions.
  A nice   B good   C calm   **D** special

8 The new café in town ___ an award for its homemade cakes.
  A won   B made   C took   D put

Speaking

12 Work in pairs. Discuss the questions.

- What did you eat for breakfast this morning?
- What did you have for dinner last night? Who cooked it? What were you doing while he / she was cooking it?
- When did you eat out last? What was the restaurant like? What was happening while you were eating your meal?
- Do you think people ate healthier food in the past? Why / Why not?

Unit 4

Awareness

1 **Which of these sentences are correct (C) and incorrect (I)?**

1 He isn't use to eating late in the evening. __I__
2 Every summer we would visit our cousins in Scotland. __C__
3 When she was young, my grandmother is used to prepare a family meal every Sunday. __I__
4 Fruit and vegetables used to be tastier. __C__
5 Did you used to like mushrooms when you were young? __I__
6 Omar and Sonia are getting used to how their new cooker works. __C__
7 I didn't use to enjoy cooking, but now I do. __C__
8 I would live in New York, but I moved to Paris last year. __I__
9 Did she use to baking her own bread when she was younger? __I__
10 Was he used to eating fast food when he lived on his own? __C__

How many did you get right? ☐

Grammar

used to and *would*

We use *used to* + infinitive for:
- actions we did regularly in the past but not now.

*My family **used to buy** fruit and vegetables from the market when I was young.*

- states that existed in the past, but that don't exist now.

*She **used to enjoy** cooking, but now she prefers eating out in restaurants.*

We use *would* + infinitive for actions we did regularly in the past but not now. We don't use it for past states
*The chef **would prepare** his favourite dish every Saturday evening.*

> **Note**
>
> We don't use *would* for questions and negatives when we talk about repeated actions in the past.
> *He **didn't use to** have breakfast.*

be used to and *get used to*

We use *be used to* + -ing form / noun to talk about something that is usual or familiar.
*My son **is used to cooking** for himself.*

We use *get used to* + -ing form / noun to talk about the process of something becoming familiar.
*We are **getting used to** spicy food. We quite like it now.*

> **Note**
>
> Be and get change depending on the tense that is needed in the context.
> *She's **used to** walking to school.*
> *Jamie **has never got used to** eating fresh fruit.*

4

Grammar exercises

2 **Tick the sentences where *used to* + infinitive can replace the past simple. Then rewrite the sentences you have ticked.**

1 He ate out a lot when he was at university. ☑
   He used to eat out a lot when he was at university.

2 I shared a house with some nurses. ☑
   I used to share a house with some nurses.

3 He changed schools last year. ☐
   _____

4 We went to lots of restaurants when we were younger. ☑
   We used to go to lots of restaurants when we were younger.

5 They arrived in London an hour ago. ☐
   _____

6 Julie had many friends when she was a student. ☑
   Julie used to have many friends when she was a student.

7 I studied hard when I was preparing for my exams. ☑
   I used to study hard when I was preparing for my exams.

8 Dean and Kate spent their holiday in Greece last summer. ☐
   _____

3 **Complete the sentences with the correct form of *used to* and the verbs.**

1 They _____*used to go*_____ (go) to a restaurant for dinner every weekend, but they don't anymore.

2 We _____*didn't use to grow*_____ (not grow) vegetables, but now we grow some every summer.

3 My aunt _____*used to drink*_____ (drink) a lot of coffee, but now she prefers tea.

4 _____*Did you use to make*_____ (you / make) your own meals?

5 Sonia and I _____*didn't use to like*_____ (not / like) each other, but now we're best friends.

6 My dad _____*used to cook*_____ (cook) dinner every night, but now he needs to work.

7 His grandparents _____*used to live*_____ (live) in a huge house, but now they live in a flat.

8 I _____*didn't use to eat*_____ (not eat) fruit, but now I eat some every day.

4

4 Rewrite the sentences with *used to* or *didn't use to*. Then tick the sentences in which you can also use *would*.

1 I have red hair now.
I didn't use to have red hair. ☐

2 They don't play football in the park after school now.
They used to play football in the park after school. ☑

3 He has a full-time job now.
He didn't use to have a full-time job. ☐

4 I like eating curries now.
I didn't use to like eating curries. ☐

5 She doesn't visit her nieces every week now.
She used to visit her nieces every week. ☑

6 We live in the city centre now.
We didn't use to live in the city centre. ☐

5 Complete the sentences with *used to* and / or *would*.

1 They _____*used to*_____ live in Mexico.

2 While on holiday, she _____*used to / would*_____ go running on the beach in the mornings.

3 He _____*used to / would*_____ take the bus home after college.

4 We _____*used to / would*_____ have picnics on nice summer days.

5 Katie _____*used to*_____ have long blonde hair.

6 When we were children, we _____*used to / would*_____ help in the garden.

7 My parents _____*used to*_____ have a cat called Biscuit.

8 My grandmother _____*used to / would*_____ bake bread every morning.

6 Read about Chan. Then use the prompts to write sentences.

> Chan moved to the UK to go to university. He didn't like it at first, but now he has got used to a lot of things in his new life.

1 live in the city centre ✓
Chan *wasn't used to living in the city centre, but he is used to it now.*

2 share a house with students ✗
Chan *hasn't got used to sharing a house with students.*

3 be away from his parents ✗
Chan *hasn't got used to being away from his parents.*

4 speak English all the time ✓
Chan *wasn't used to speaking in English all the time, but he is used to it now.*

5 cook his own meals ✓
Chan *wasn't used to cooking his own meals, but he is used to it now.*

6 the new culture ✓
Chan *wasn't used to the new culture, but he is used to it now.*

7 drive on the left side of the road ✗
Chan *hasn't got used to driving on the left side of the road.*

8 the rainy weather ✗
Chan *hasn't got used to the rainy weather.*

7 Choose the correct option (a–c) to complete the sentences.

1 Eloise ___ to have short black hair.
   a would
   b is used
   (c) used

2 'I've never used this cooker before.'
   'Don't worry; you'll soon ___ to it.'
   (a) get used
   b be used
   c used

3 ___ work in that restaurant?
   a Did Tom get use to
   (b) Did Tom use to
   c Did Tom used to

4 Theresa ___ getting up early.
   a wouldn't
   b didn't use to
   (c) isn't used to

5 My grandad couldn't use the laptop at first, but he ___ to it.
   a used to
   (b) got used
   c got use

6 She's slowly ___ to life in the big city.
   a got use
   (b) getting used
   c used

7 Mum ___ always tell us a story before bed.
   a was used to
   (b) would
   c got used to

8 Grant ___ have a dog.
   (a) didn't use to
   b didn't use
   c didn't used to

Vocabulary

Word formation

8 Complete the table.

Noun	Verb	Adjective
boredom	bore	1 _boring / bored_
brightness	brighten	2 _bright_
comfort	3 _comfort_	comfortable / uncomfortable
creativity	create	4 _creative_
5 _custom / customer_	customise	customary
6 _freshness_	freshen	fresh
friend	befriend	7 _friendly / unfriendly_
locality	localise	8 _local_
sustainability	9 _sustain_	sustainable
trend	trend	10 _trendy_

9 Complete the sentences with words from Exercise 8.

1 I used to go to a _trendy_ restaurant, but I got annoyed with the tiny portions!
2 We prefer eating in _local_ restaurants that are easy to get to.
3 My parents are worried about food _sustainability_ , so now they eat less meat.
4 She was excited to try the new café, but the waiter was really _unfriendly_ .
5 My grandad would always buy my grandma _fresh_ flowers every week.
6 The _customer_ at the end of the long queue was starting to feel a bit ill.
7 My brother is very tall, so he finds travelling by plane _uncomfortable_ .
8 _Bright_ sunshine always makes me feel happy.
9 The service at the restaurant was slow, and the children started to get _bored_ .
10 You can test the _freshness_ of an egg by putting it in water. If it sinks – don't eat it!

4

Exam practice

10 **For each question, write the correct answer. Write one word for each gap.**

1 Did your grandfather ___use___ to grow his own vegetables?

2 My sister ___would___ come home, have her dinner and go to her room.

3 The food is a bit unusual here, but I think I'm slowly ___getting___ used to it.

4 Sara isn't used ___to___ eating spicy food, so I'm not sure about serving this curry.

5 We always ___used___ to roast a chicken at the weekend.

6 ___Were___ you used to eating late when you lived in the city?

7 We did ___not___ use to eat fish, but we do now.

8 Lola and Tim ___are___ used to having a cooked breakfast on Sunday mornings. They love them!

Multiple-choice cloze

11 **For each question, choose the correct answer.**

1 Dad was ___ the meat on the BBQ when it started to rain.

   A frying   **(B)** grilling   **C** boiling   **D** baking

2 This coffee is too ___ . Can I have some sugar, please?

   A salty   **B** sweet   **C** sour   **(D)** bitter

3 We need a ___ of tuna to make this salad.

   A box   **(B)** tin   **C** bowl   **D** glass

4 Every week we buy a big ___ of bananas.

   (A) bunch   **B** jar   **C** portion   **D** jug

5 I'm a terrible cook. My food always tastes absolutely ___ .

   (A) disgusting   **B** tasty   **C** delicious   **D** special

6 The décor of the restaurant was so ___ everything was grey!

   A colourful   **B** expensive   **C** bright   **(D)** dull

7 Everything is on the table; all we need are the knives and ___ to eat with.

   A cups   **B** saucers   **(C)** forks   **D** mugs

8 I need a ___ to eat my soup with.

   (A) spoon   **B** pot   **C** bottle   **D** knife

Writing

12 **Read the writing task and write your answer in about 100 words. Try to use different adjectives.**

You and your friends went to a trendy restaurant in your town at the weekend and you were very happy with the meal. Write an article about the restaurant for your school magazine, giving your opinion about it and saying why you recommend it.

Grammar

1 Complete the sentences with the present simple or present continuous form of the verbs.

1 Mum _____is seeing_____ (see) the doctor about her headaches at two o'clock this afternoon.
2 Billy can't go to the cinema because he _____'s studying_____ . He _____studies_____ (study) every evening during the week.
3 _____Do they usually_____ (they / usually / call) you before they come to your house?
4 Linda _____is running_____ (run) in the park at the moment. She _____goes_____ (go) for a run every morning before she _____has_____ (have) breakfast.
5 My family _____gets_____ (get) an email from Jane once a week. She _____'s cycling_____ (cycle) around France and _____always remembers_____ (always / remember) to keep in touch.
6 Lewis _____thinks_____ (think) maths is very difficult. He _____doesn't seem_____ (not / seem) to know the answers to simple questions.
7 Look! It _____'s snowing_____ (snow). It _____rarely snows_____ (rarely / snow) in Scotland at this time of the year.
8 When I _____do_____ (do) well in school, I _____feel_____ (feel) very happy.
9 My grandparents _____are staying_____ (stay) with us tonight.
10 My dad _____is forever complaining_____ (forever / complain) about the music I play.

2 Complete the sentences with one word for each gap.

1 I made _____a_____ tuna sandwich for my lunch.
2 I want to make a cake, so I need a _____bag_____ of flour and a box of eggs.
3 She has a problem. Can you give her _____some_____ advice?
4 I bought a _____few_____ apples at the market.
5 We need a _____lot_____ of milk to make pancakes. I'll go to the supermarket.
6 It's Saturday! I've got _____lots_____ of time to do what I want.
7 I _____am_____ getting annoyed with that loud music!
8 How _____many_____ people were at your family get-together last weekend?
9 There isn't _____any_____ food in the fridge; it's completely empty!
10 Could I have a _____little_____ sugar for my tea, please?

3 Choose the correct option to complete the sentences.

1 *Were you cooking* / *Did you cook* when your dad arrived home?
2 The cook *made* / *was making* the soup, tasted it and added some salt.
3 *Did they go* / *Were they going* to that new restaurant last Sunday?
4 I *wasn't having* / *didn't have* time for lunch today!
5 My brother *didn't get* / *wasn't getting* here an hour ago; he's been here all morning.
6 Dad *watered* / *was watering* the flowers while Mum was planting some vegetables.
7 Kevin *was frying* / *fried* onions when he burned his hand.
8 The sun *was shining* / *shone* and the children were playing happily in the park.
9 I *believed* / *was believing* him when he promised to study more.
10 Jan *was never eating* / *never ate* cooked lunches at school.

4 Choose the correct option (a–b) to complete the sentences.

1 Theo looks different. He ___ have red hair and now it's blond!
   a would
   (b) used to

2 'I don't know how use this new laptop.'
  'It's easy; you'll soon ___ to it.'
   a used
   (b) get used

3 '___ be a chef at Chez Canard?'
   (a) Did your father use to
   b Did your father get used to

4 I know that woman. She ___ to teach me maths at college.
   a would
   (b) used

5 William ___ getting up late in the mornings – he always wakes up at six o'clock.
   (a) isn't used to
   b didn't use to

6 My dad didn't like the new cooker at first, but he ___ to it.
   a used
   (b) got used

7 'How is Tony doing at university?'
  'Fine. He's slowly ___ it.'
   (a) getting used to
   b being used to

8 Grandma ___ always make pancakes for breakfast.
   a was used to
   (b) would

9 My sister ___ live on her own, but she does now.
   a isn't getting used to
   (b) didn't use to

10 We ___ have a pet, but now we've got a cat.
   (a) didn't use to
   b didn't used to

5 Choose the correct option to complete the sentences.

1 Grandad *is always making* / |*always makes*| lunch at twelve o'clock on Sundays.
2 My father *got used to* / |*used to*| work in a restaurant when he was younger.
3 Celia likes a *few* / |*little*| honey in her tea.
4 What time |*does the film start*| / *is the filming starting* this evening?
5 Can I have a |*glass*| / *loaf* of milk, please?
6 We went into the garden and we |*had*| / *were having* a barbecue.
7 They were eating breakfast *while* / |*when*| my uncle's phone rang.
8 My grandfather *is speaking* / |*speaks*| three languages.
9 Tim *is never getting used to* / |*has never got used*| to the smell of onions.
10 There aren't any |*biscuits*| / *cake* in the cupboard.

6 Tick the correct sentences. Then correct the mistakes.

1 My cousin Jim stays with us for the weekend.
   My cousin Jim is staying with us for the weekend.

2 Would you like a fruit, Billy?
   Would you like some fruit, Billy?

3 His feet is very big!
   His feet are very big!

4 Peter visits Aunt Kate twice a month.
   ✓

5 There wasn't many rain last summer.
   There wasn't much rain last summer.

6 Was the cook working in his kitchen all day?
   ✓

Use of English

Sentence transformation

7 Complete the second sentence so that it has a similar meaning to the first sentence, using the word given. Do not change the word given. You must use between two and five words.

1 My cousin played a lot of sports when he was younger.

My cousin _____*used to play*_____ a lot of sports when he was younger. **PLAY**

2 Dad never watched TV when he was younger.

When he was younger, Dad _____*didn't / did not use to*_____ watch TV. **TO**

3 Grant has an appointment to see his lawyer on Friday.

Grant _____*is seeing*_____ his lawyer on Friday. **IS**

4 Amal has just moved to the city, so he finds it quite strange.

Amal _*isn't / is not used to*_ living in the city. **USED**

5 Shall I put milk in your tea?

Do you _____*want some milk*_____ in your tea? **SOME**

6 Does this restaurant serve vegetarian dishes?

Are _____*there any vegetarian dishes*_____ on the menu in this restaurant? **ANY**

7 Our manager complains about our work all the time.

Our manager _____*is continually complaining*_____ about our work. **CONTINUALLY**

8 I haven't got much time to spend with you today.

I've only got _____*a little time*_____ to spend with you today. **A**

9 Tom started to work on his project at seven o'clock and he finished at ten o'clock.

Tommy _____*was working from*_____ seven o'clock to ten o'clock. **WORKING**

10 They arrived for lunch. Grandad was asleep.

Grandad _*was sleeping when*_ they arrived for lunch. **SLEEPING**

Word formation

8 Use the word in capitals to form a word that fits in the gap.

1 Look at all the wonderful fruit and vegetables. They look so _*colourful*_! **COLOUR**

2 This soup is a bit _*tasteless*_. Is there any salt in it? **TASTE**

3 They became vegetarian so that the food they ate was more _____*sustainable*_____. **SUSTAIN**

4 Their children are very _*creative*_; they can paint, draw and play the guitar! **CREATE**

5 Fast-food restaurants offer mainly _*processed*_ food. **PROCESS**

6 There's a _*trendy*_ new gift shop in town – do you want to go? **TREND**

7 That supermarket has good quality food that's _____*inexpensive*_____. **EXPENSIVE**

8 I can always call my best friend when I need some help or advice. She's very _*reliable*_. **RELY**

Grammar

9 For questions 1–10, choose the word or phrase that best completes the sentence.

1 Why ___ talking during lessons? It's rude!
A   always are you
B   you do always
C   are you always
D   you always

2 How ___ slices of cake do you want?
A   much
B   some
C   any
D   many

3 What time ___ on TV tonight, Dad?
A   does the cookery show start
B   is the cookery show starting
C   did the cookery show start
D   the cookery show starts

4 We were making salad sandwiches when we ___ there weren't any tomatoes.
A   are remembering
B   remembered
C   were remembering
D   was remembering

5 Charlie ___ to the dentist yesterday.
A   was going
B   is going
C   wasn't going
D   went

6 I ___ of making pasta for lunch this Sunday.
A   am thinking
B   think
C   thinking
D   don't think

7 My aunt and uncle ___ with us at the moment.
A   stayed
B   are staying
C   stay
D   staying

8 My friend Bonnie ___ got three brothers.
A   has
B   is having
C   was having
D   was

9 Grandma ___ to live alone, but she does now.
A   used to
B   wasn't used
C   isn't used
D   didn't use

10 We found ___ information about the festival on the internet.
A   an
B   much
C   many
D   some

Vocabulary

10 For questions 11–20, choose the word or phrase that best completes the sentence.

11 My older brothers always get annoyed ___ me.
A   with
B   of
C   for
D   to

12 My best friend is ___ married next week.
A   keeping
B   having
C   getting
D   going

13 He was brought up ___ his aunt and uncle.
A   by
B   for
C   to
D   of

14 The cook cut ___ all the vegetables.
A   in
B   down
C   out
D   up

15 Put the potatoes in water and ___ them.
A   fry
B   boil
C   grill
D   roast

16 Ben wants to ___ with Eva.
A   split up
B   put on
C   speak up
D   put up

17 I can't drink this coffee – it's too ___ .
A   spicy
B   sour
C   bitter
D   salty

18 Can you buy a ___ of bananas from the shop?
A   slice
B   bunch
C   tin
D   packet

19 The athlete ___ a world record.
A   reduced
B   won
C   found
D   broke

20 I applied ___ twenty jobs before I got one!
A   for
B   with
C   to
D   in

1 **Which of these sentences are correct (C) and incorrect (I)?**

1 We have been damaging the environment for centuries!   _C_

2 Scientists have discovered a new kind of insect in December.   _I_

3 The zoo just closed for the day.   _I_

4 Has she been recycling her rubbish for a long time?   _C_

5 They have been doing research since 2010.   _C_

6 We haven't been living here since five years.   _I_

7 I have studied marine life last year.   _I_

8 How long have you been travelling in Asia?   _C_

9 Dr Fossey has been to Kenya; she'll be back next month.   _I_

10 We have had five terrible storms so far this winter.   _C_

How many did you get right? ☐

Grammar

Present perfect simple

Affirmative	Negative	Questions
I / We / You / They **have** (**'ve**) look**ed**. He / She/ It **has** (**'s**) look**ed**.	I / We / You / They **have not** (**haven't**) look**ed**. He / She / It **has not** (**hasn't**) look**ed**.	**Have** I / we / you / they look**ed**? **Has** he / she / it look**ed**?
Short Answers		
Yes, I / we / you / they have. **Yes**, he / she / it has.	**No**, I / we / you / they **haven't**. **No**, he / she / it **hasn't**.	

Spelling: talk → talk**ed**, place → plac**ed**, travel → trave**lled**, tidy → ti**died**, stay → stay**ed**

We use the present perfect simple for:
- actions that have just finished.
*The fisherman **has just caught** a fish.*

- experiences and achievements.
*The scientist **has won** many awards.*

- something that started in the past and has continued until now.
*The marine biologists **have studied** the reef since 2018.*

- something that happened in the past, but we don't know or we don't say exactly when.
*Researchers **have discovered** a new problem.*

- something that happened in the past and has a result that affects the present.
*Hunting **has endangered** many animals on the planet.*

> **Note**
>
> Some verbs are irregular and do not follow these spelling rules. See a list of irregular verbs on pages 158–159.

> **Note**
>
> We often use these common time expressions with the present perfect simple: *already, before, ever, for, for a long time / ages, just, never, once, recently, since 2017 / June, so far, twice, three times, until now, yet,* etc.
> *The vet has worked with monkeys **since** 2015.*

have been and *have gone*

Notice the difference between *have been* and *have gone*.
have been = someone has gone somewhere and has now returned.   *We **have been** to Australia. It's amazing!*
have gone = someone has gone somewhere and is still there.   *Peter is not here. He **has gone** to the museum.*

ago, for and *since*

We often use *ago* with the past simple, and *for* and *since* with the present perfect simple. We use *ago* at the end of a sentence with the past simple.
*I **went** to the beach two weeks **ago**.*

We use *for* + a phrase for a period of time at the end of the sentence with the present perfect simple.
*They **have lived** in Venezuela **for** ten years.*

We use *since* with a point in time in the past at the end of sentence with the present perfect simple.
*The Caspian tiger **has been** extinct **since** the 1970s.*

Present perfect simple and past simple

We use the present perfect simple when we talk about something that happened in the past and has a result that affects the present. We also use the present perfect simple when we don't know or we don't say when something happened in the past.

We use the past simple when we say when something happened.
*Industrial activity **has affected** our climate.*
*She **has travelled** all over the world. They **visited** New Zealand **last year**.*

Present perfect continuous

Affirmative	Negative	Questions
I / We / You / They **have ('ve) been** look**ing**. He / She / It **has ('s) been** look**ing**.	I / We / You / They **have not (haven't) been** looking. He / She / It **has not (hasn't) been** look**ing**.	**Have** I / we / you / they **been** looking? **Has** he / she / it **been** looking?
Short Answers		
Yes, I / we / you / they **have**. **Yes**, he / she / it **has**.	**No**, I / we / you / they **haven't**. **No**, he / she / it **hasn't**.	

Spelling: take → tak**ing**, swim → swi**mming**, study → stu**dying**

We use the present perfect continuous:
- for actions that started in the past and are still in progress now or have happened repeatedly until now.
*The team of scientists **has been looking** for new butterflies on the island.*
- for actions that happened repeatedly in the past and have finished recently, but that have results that affect the present.
*I've got a headache because I **have been studying** for hours.*
- to emphasise how long actions have been in progress for.
*My uncle **has been exploring** forests for twenty years.*

> **Note**
>
> We often use these common time expressions with the present perfect continuous: *all day / night / week, for years / a long time / ages, lately, recently, since.*
> We can use *How long ...?* with the present perfect continuous in questions and *for (very) long* in questions and negative sentences.
> *I have been working on this science project **all day**.*
> ***How long** has Martha been working as a biologist?*
> *We haven't been searching for new species **for very long**. It's only been three months.*

Present perfect simple and present perfect continuous

We use the present perfect simple to talk about something we have done or achieved, or an action that is complete. It is also used to say how many times something happened.
She **has read** that science magazine three times in the last week.

We use the present perfect continuous to talk about how long something has been happening. It is not important whether or not it has finished.
They **have been talking** about climate change for hours.

Grammar exercises

2 Complete the sentences with the past simple or present perfect simple form of the verbs.

1 **A:** ___Have you seen___ (you / see) Dr Stevens?
B: Actually, she ___'s just left___ (just / leave).

2 **A:** I ___haven't felt well___ (not / feel) well since I got back from holiday.
B: Well, ___have you made___ (you / make) an appointment with the doctor yet?

3 **A:** ___Have you had___ (you / have) any news from Maria?
B: Yes, she ___called___ (call) me from Brazil yesterday.

4 **A:** I think Peter ___has bought___ (buy) new snorkelling equipment.
B: Yes, he ___bought___ (buy) some last week.

5 **A:** ___Has she given___ (she / give) money to the wildlife charity yet?
B: Yes, she ___sent___ (send) some this morning.

6 **A:** ___Have they talked___ (they / talk) to their science teacher?
B: Yes, they ___talked___ (talk) to her yesterday, after school.

7 **A:** How long ___has Petra worked___ (Petra / work) as a biologist?
B: She ___'s worked___ (work) as a biologist for five years.

8 **A:** ___Have they visited___ (they / visit) Australia?
B: Many times. In fact, they ___went___ (go) in January.

3 Use the prompts to write sentences with the present perfect simple.

1 I / already / see / the coral reefs.
I've already seen the coral reefs.

2 Tina / move / house / yet?
Has Tina moved house yet?

3 we / already / walk / ten kilometres / today
We've already walked ten kilometres today.

4 Jack / never / travel / to France
Jack has never travelled to France.

5 the train / just / arrive / at the station
The train has just arrived at the station.

6 you / ever / meet / any famous explorers?
Have you ever met any famous explorers?

7 she / try / snorkelling / before?
Has she tried snorkelling before?

8 they / not finish / their research / yet
They haven't finished their research yet.

5

4 Complete the sentences with have / has been or have / has gone.

1 We _____'ve been_____ to California twice so far this year, but we want to go back again.
2 You can't see Sam before Sunday. He _____'s gone_____ on a research trip.
3 Martha _____has been_____ to the White Cliffs of Dover many times.
4 Karl and Beth _____have gone_____ to Argentina for a few weeks. They're coming back next month.
5 Grant _____has gone_____ to the library. He's coming back for lunch.
6 The biologist _____has gone_____ into the jungle and won't be back for hours.
7 I _____'ve been_____ to the coast three times this week.
8 Tony and Ben aren't here right now. They _____'ve gone_____ into town to buy some food.

5 Choose the correct option to complete the sentences.

1 They haven't reached the top of the mountain ever / *yet*.
2 Have you for / *just* arrived?
3 The elephant has yet / *already* had its lunch.
4 It hasn't rained in Morocco just / *for* months.
5 We became interested in endangered animals three years *ago* / already.
6 He hasn't been to the rainforest for / *since* last year.
7 Has Paul yet / *ever* heard a talk by that scientist?
8 I haven't seen my brother since / *for* weeks.

6 Complete the sentences with the present perfect simple or present perfect continuous form of the verbs.

1 A: You look ill, Julia!
   B: I know. I _____haven't felt / haven't been feeling_____ (not / feel) well since the weekend.
2 A: Is Fran in the garden?
   B: Yes, she _____'s been watching_____ (watch) the birds all morning.
3 A: Do you like your new teacher?
   B: Oh yes! She's one of the most interesting people I _____'ve ever met_____ (ever / meet).
4 A: Are you still working on your project?
   B: No, I _____'ve just finished it_____ (just / finish) it.
5 A: Your English is very good.
   B: Thank you. I _____'ve been learning_____ (learn) it since I was very young.
6 A: How long _____have you been working_____ (you / work) here?
   B: For three weeks now.
7 A: Are Dean and Ana still here?
   B: No, they _____'ve already left_____ (already / leave).
8 A: Is this your first visit to the Amazon?
   B: Yes, we _____'ve never been_____ (never / be) here before.

7 Find one mistake in each sentence. Then correct the mistakes.

1 Have they ever see an iceberg?
   Have they ever seen an iceberg?

2 Lynn and I finish university last year.
   Lynn and I finished university last year.

3 We've moved to this city five year ago.
   We moved to this city five years ago.

4 Nancy is lived in Peru for two months now.
   Nancy has lived / has been living in Peru for two months now.

5 They've make a lot of mistakes.
   They've made a lot of mistakes.

6 The scientist has went to look at the stream.
   The scientist has gone to look at the stream.

7 Jake hasn't finished his research just.
   Jack hasn't finished his research yet.

8 I already done my maths homework.
   I've already done my maths homework.

Vocabulary

Prepositions

8 Complete the sentences with these prepositions.

at   before   for   from   in (x2)   into   onto   to (x2)

1 Governments need to do something about pollution ___before___ it's too late.
2 They've been doing their research ___for___ ten years now.
3 In Australia, you can do everything ___from___ snorkelling to visiting deserts.
4 They want to turn the land ___into___ a wildlife centre.
5 He threw rubbish ___onto___ the beach.
6 The explorers took three days to climb from the bottom ___to___ the top of the mountain.
7 An unidentified object appeared ___in___ the sky.
8 The ship is ___in___ the middle of the Pacific Ocean.
9 We took the children ___to___ a science museum at the weekend.
10 I'm very busy ___at___ the moment.

Word formation

9 Use the word in capitals to form a word that fits in the gap.

1 We can get ___renewable___ energy from the sun, the wind and waves. **RENEW**
2 The ___inventor___ designed a device to collect rubbish in the ocean. **INVENT**
3 Put the plastic in the blue ___recycling___ bin. **RECYCLE**
4 Many take-away coffee cups are now ___biodegradable___ . **BIODEGRADE**
5 Marine life can't ___survive___ in polluted water. **SURVIVAL**
6 The ___electricity___ we use in our home comes from wind power. **ELECTRIC**
7 The Amazon River is ___visible___ from space. **VISION**
8 Our climate is getting ___warmer___ and this causes droughts and floods. **WARMTH**

5

Exam practice

10 For each question, choose the correct answer.

1 They believe the explorers entered the dark ___ and got lost.
   A cliff   **(B) cave**   C beach   D river

2 The world's ___ are melting with worrying speed.
   (A) glaciers   B valleys   C rainforests   D oceans

3 We can get cold fresh water from that ___ .
   A reef   **(B) stream**   C iceberg   D coast

4 From the top of the mountain, we had a fantastic view of the ___ below.
   A climate   B bottom   C floor   **(D) valley**

5 The ___ is disappearing because of intensive farming.
   (A) rainforest   B cliff   C ocean   D glacier

6 My dream is to live in a house on the ___ of Scotland.
   A river   B cave   **(C) coast**   D reef

7 Don't go too near the edge of the ___ ; it's a long way down!
   A stream   B jungle   C valley   **(D) cliff**

8 ___ energy comes from the sun.
   A Fossil   B Fuel   **(C) Solar**   D Power

11 For each question, write the correct answer. Write one word for each gap.

1 The fisherman has __*caught*__ 20 kilos of fish so far this morning.
2 She studied marine __*biology*__ at university.
3 I've __*already*__ emptied the rubbish bins, but I haven't done the recycling bins yet.
4 He's worked at the power station __*since*__ 2019.
5 We need to stop using __*fossil*__ fuels and start using more solar and wind power.
6 She hasn't eaten any meat for a long __*time*__ .
7 __*Did*__ you see any sharks when you went snorkelling last year?
8 The astronauts have __*been*__ living on the space station for a few months now.

Speaking

12 Work in pairs. Discuss these things with your partner.

- two things you have / haven't done this week
- one thing you've done to help the environment this month
- two things you've been doing for the past few years that help to protect the environment

1 Which of these sentences are correct (C) and incorrect (I)?

1 Can Toby play a piano? ___I___
2 Jake is in hospital until Friday. ___C___
3 The zoo has got an elephant. The elephant is from India. ___C___
4 The Pindus Mountains are in Europe. ___C___
5 The Greeks are very proud of their history. ___C___
6 Do you have to wear an uniform to work? ___I___
7 The scientists have a meeting once the week. ___I___
8 She is a best biologist in the country. ___I___
9 A sun rises in the east and sets in the west. ___I___
10 I watch TV in the evening. ___C___

How many did you get right?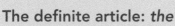

Grammar

The indefinite article: *a / an*

We use a before a consonant sound.
a cave   a university
We use an before a vowel sound.
an elephant   an aeroplane

We use *a / an*:
- with singular countable nouns.
*She always has **a book** with her.*
- to mean per / each in expressions of frequency.
*The biologists meet once **a** month.*
- to mention something for the first time.
***A** bird appeared in our garden.*
- to show job, status, etc.
*She is **an** explorer.*

The definite article: *the*

We use the with singular and plural countable nouns and uncountable nouns to talk about something specific when the noun is mentioned for a second time.
*Look! There's a shark in the ocean. **The** shark looks huge.*

We also use *the* before:
- unique nouns.
***The** Earth is about 71 per cent water.*
- names of cinemas, theatres, ships, hotels, etc.
*Where did they build **the** Titanic?*
*They're staying at **the** Strand Hotel.*
- names of rivers, deserts, mountain ranges, and names or nouns with *of*.
*Where is **the** Gobi Desert?*
***The** King of Spain is on an official visit.*
- countries or groups of countries whose names are plural.
*Is **the** USA bigger than Canada?*
*We come from **the** Bahamas.*
- play + musical instruments.
*Alice plays **the** guitar and **the** piano.*
- nationalities.
***The** Scottish are well-known for their friendliness.*
***The** Japanese have an interesting culture.*

- adjectives used as nouns.

The young want governments to do more to save the planet.

- superlatives.

*The green anaconda is **the** largest snake in the world.*

- the following words: *beach, countryside, station, jungle,* etc.

*It isn't warm enough to go to **the** beach today.*

- *morning, afternoon, evening.*

*Many people go to work in **the** morning.*

We do not use *the* before:

- proper nouns.

*Is **Jimmy** at school today?*

- names of sports, games, colours, days, months, drinks, holidays, meals and languages (not followed by the word *language*).

Yellow is my mother's favourite colour.

- subjects of study.

*I find **maths** very difficult.*

- names of countries, cities, streets (BUT: *the high street*), squares, bridges (BUT: *the Golden Gate Bridge*), parks, stations, individual mountains, islands, lakes, continents.

*Glasgow is a large city in **Scotland**.*

- bed, school, hospital, prison, university, college, court when we talk about something related to the main purpose of the place. (*Work* never takes *the*.)

*Karl is at **school**. (He's a student there.)*

*Karl's mum has gone to **the school** to see his teacher. (She isn't a student; she's gone to visit someone.)*

- means of transportation in expressions like by plane, etc. (BUT: *on **the** plane*).

*We decided to go to Australia by **ship**.*

Grammar exercises

2 Write *a* or *an*.

1	*a* station	6	*a* uniform
2	*an* hour	7	*a* reef
3	*an* onion	8	*a* house
4	*an* island	9	*an* airport
5	*an* umbrella	10	*a* fish

3 Complete the sentences with *a*, *an* or *the*.

1 ____*The*____ reading group gets together twice ____*a*____ month to discuss books.

2 ____*The*____ president of our college is also ____*an*____ artist.

3 Aunt Beth has gone to ____*the*____ school to collect Joe – he's feeling ill.

4 I saw ____*an*____ octopus on the ocean floor. ____*The*____ octopus suddenly changed colour!

5 I think I'll go to ____*the*____ high street because I need ____*a*____ new umbrella.

6 ____*The*____ moon is very bright tonight.

7 ____*A*____ friend told me he stayed at ____*the*____ Hilton once.

8 We need to help ____*the*____ homeless.

4 Choose the correct option to complete the sentences.

1 *The biology /* Biology *is my brother's favourite subject.*
2 Does that archaeologist come from *Philippines /* the Philippines ?
3 What time do you usually have *the breakfast /* breakfast ?
4 Has anyone ever been able to climb *the Mount Etna /* Mount Etna ?
5 I usually do volunteer work on *the Saturday /* Saturday .
6 Is *the Doctor Jones /* Doctor Jones going to the conference?
7 Did you play football */ the football* when you were a student?
8 I believe Rachel Carson was the best */ best* marine biologist ever.
9 Most of the scientists will travel to Peru by plane */ the plane.*
10 We're going to the coast */ coast* to clean up some beaches.

5 Complete the sentences with these words and *the* where necessary. Use each word twice.

bed   court   hospital   prison   school

1 He's going to ____court____ today with his lawyer.
2 Please, tell ____the court____ what happened that night.
3 I'm very tired and I'm going to ____bed____ .
4 If you're looking for your snorkelling equipment, it's on ____the bed____ .
5 Is that ____the prison____ where Oscar Wilde was a prisoner?
6 She's in ____prison____ for stealing money from the company.
7 Many people were hurt in the car accident and were taken to ____hospital____ .
8 My sister has just had an operation, so I'm going to ____the hospital____ to see her.
9 If you're walking past ____the school____ , can you give this letter to Mrs James?
10 Do you think Tom will go to university once he finishes ____school____ ?

6 Complete the conversations with *a, an, the* or – (no article).

1 A: Did you stay in ____a____ hotel when you went to Athens?
   B: Yes. I had ____a____ nice room in ____the____ Hilton.
2 A: What did you have for ____–____ lunch at ____–____ school today?
   B: I had ____a____ sandwich and ____an____ apple.
3 A: How often do you take ____a____ holiday?
   B: I try to have a break three times ____a____ year.
4 A: Did you go to ____the____ Playhouse Theatre last night?
   B: Yes, it was ____an____ amazing evening and the play was ____the____ best I've ever seen.
5 A: Have you got ____a____ car?
   B: No, but I've got ____a____ bike. ____The____ bike I've got is new.
6 A: That's ____an____ interesting painting.
   B: Yes, it is. ____An____ artist from Italy painted it.
7 A: Did you enjoy your trip to ____–____ Europe?
   B: Yes, I loved Paris and seeing ____the____ Eiffel Tower and ____the____ Louvre Museum.
8 A: Do you play ____–____ tennis?
   B: Yes, I do. I often play with ____the____ history teacher at ____the____ school where I work.

6

Sentence transformation

7 Complete the second sentence so that it has a similar meaning to the first sentence, using the word given. Do not change the word given. You must use between two and five words.

1 It's a shame that so many high-street shops are closing.

   It's a shame that so many shops _____ *on the high street* _____ are closing. **THE**

2 I believe no land mammal in the world is heavier than the African bush elephant.

   I think _____ *the heaviest land mammal* _____ in the world is the African bush elephant. **HEAVIEST**

3 Our action group meets on Mondays and Wednesdays every week.

   Our action group meets _____ *twice a week* _____ on Mondays and Wednesdays. **A**

4 She works in court in London.

   She _____ *works as a lawyer* _____ in the London courts. **LAWYER**

5 Jay is off from school today – he's unwell.

   Jay _____ *isn't / is not at school* _____ today – he's unwell. **NOT**

6 At the weekend she acts at the local theatre.

   At the weekend _____ *she's / she is / works as an actor* _____ at the local theatre. **ACTOR**

7 I don't like travelling by plane – I get very nervous.

   I don't like travelling _____ *on a plane* _____ – I get very nervous. **ON**

8 I've been studying every week night because I've got exams.

   I've been studying in _____ *the evening during the* _____ week because I've got exams. **EVENING**

Vocabulary

Collocations and expressions

8 Complete the collocations with these verbs.

clean up	land	organise	reduce	recycle	take	talk to	write

1 _*talk to*_ your friends and family

2 _*organise*_ local events

3 _*clean up*_ a park

4 _*recycle*_ plastic

5 _*write*_ a blog

6 _*take*_ public transport

7 _*reduce*_ your use of electricity

8 _*land*_ a plane

9 Complete the sentences with the correct form of the collocations from Exercise 8.

1 Why don't they _____ *organise local events* _____ to help new people meet other members of their community?

2 I'm going to _____ *clean up a park* _____ near your house on Saturday. Do you want to come and help?

3 He _*reduced his use of electricity*_ by washing his clothes at a lower temperature.

4 She's been _____ *writing a blog* _____ about her life as an explorer for many years.

5 It's helpful to _____ *recycle plastic* _____ , but we also need to reduce our use of these products.

6 My mum hates driving, so we're used to _____ *taking public transport* _____ or walking everywhere!

7 Have you ever seen a pilot _____ *land a plane* _____ on water?

8 She's worried about moving school, so she's going to _____ *talk to her friends and family* _____ about it.

Exam practice

Open cloze

10 For each question, write the correct answer. Write one word for each gap.

1 Lonesome George was a giant tortoise that lived in _____*the*_____ Galápagos Islands.

2 If we don't _____*take*_____ action now, the Earth won't survive.

3 Do you know what the _____*most*_____ common language on the planet is?

4 Some recycled waste can be turned _____*into*_____ fuel to heat our homes.

5 I read _____*an*_____ interesting article about spiders yesterday.

6 The wildlife park has every animal you can think of, _____*from*_____ cows to lions!

7 My uncle is travelling _____*at*_____ the moment.

8 She _____*plays*_____ the piano and the violin.

Multiple-choice cloze

11 For each question, choose the correct answer.

1 She wants to set ___ an after-school club on Mondays.
A out   (B) up   C in   D to

2 Hans and I travelled to the mountains by ___ train.
(A) –   B a   C the   D an

3 The ___ from cars and planes is really bad in this area.
A power   B fuels   C energy   (D) pollution

4 I read ___ amazing article about icebergs last night.
A the   B a   (C) an   D –

5 My brother is named ___ our grandad.
(A) after   B for   C to   D with

6 The sun and wind are sources of energy that can never run ___ .
A to   B on   (C) out   D in

7 There are probably many species of fish on the ocean floor that ___ world doesn't know about.
A an   (B) the   C a   D –

8 Corals aren't plants – they are made up ___ tiny animals.
A in   B around   C for   (D) of

Writing

12 Read the writing task and write your answer in about 100 words. Try to use a friendly greeting and ending, questions and informal expressions.

Write an email to your friend about an event in your town that helped the environment. Say what you liked about the event the most and why.

1 **Which of these sentences are correct (C) and incorrect (I)?**

1 My father is a man whose easy to talk to. ⊥

2 Como, that is in Italy, is a lovely place. ⊥

3 How expensive was the necklace who was stolen? ⊥

4 The friendship I have with my sister is something which I could not live without. C

5 That's the building where my mother used to work. C

6 Tuesday, 2nd September, was the day when I met my best friend. C

7 That is the restaurant that my parents took me for my birthday. ⊥

8 Gina is a person that never wears trainers. C

9 Jake, who lives next door to me, used to be my hairdresser. C

10 My uncle, who name is Joe, is very reliable. ⊥

How many did you get right? ☐

Grammar

Relative clauses

Relative clauses give more information about the subject or the object of a sentence. They are introduced by the following words (relative pronouns):

- *who* for people.
*The film is about a girl **who** wants to work in fashion.*
- *which* for things.
*The book, **which** was about a young explorer, was fantastic.*
- *whose* to show possession.
*The orangutan, **whose** name is Suryia, lives in the USA.*
- *when* for time.
*A holiday is a time **when** people relax.*
- *where* for places.
*This is the farm **where** you can feed some of the animals.*

Defining relative clauses

This type of relative clause gives us information that we need to be able to understand who or what the speaker is talking about. We do not use commas to separate it from the rest of the sentence. We can use *that* instead of *who* and *which* in defining relative clauses.
*These are the people **who** / **that** help the homeless.*

In defining relative clauses, we can omit the relative pronoun when it is the object in the relative clause.
This is the girl (that) Emma told you about. (In the relative clause, *Emma* is the subject of the verb *told* and *that* is the object.)
This is the girl that told Emma about you. (In the relative clause, *that* is the subject of the verb *told* and *Emma* is the object.)

Non-defining relative clauses

This type of relative clause gives us extra information which isn't necessary to understand who or what we are talking about. We use commas to separate it from the rest of the sentence.
In non-defining relative clauses, we can never omit the relative pronoun.
*His mother, **who** is a teacher, works with young children.*

Grammar exercises

2 **Use the prompts to write sentences. Use *who*, *which* or *where*.**

1 laptop / something / we use to do our work
  A laptop is something which we use to do our work.

2 library / place / we borrow books
  A library is a place where we borrow books.

3 firefighter / person / puts out fires
  A firefighter is a person who puts out fires.

4 tablet / device / we use to watch videos
  A tablet is a device which we use to watch videos.

5 zoo / place / we can see animals
  A zoo is a place where we can see animals.

6 architect / person / designs buildings
  An architect is a person who designs buildings.

7 watch / a piece of jewellery / we use to tell the time
  A watch is a piece of jewellery which we use to tell the time.

8 elephant / animal / live in Asia and Africa
  An elephant is an animal which lives in Asia and Africa.

3 **Match the beginnings of the sentences (1–8) with their endings (a–h).**

1	Stella is the fashion designer	g	a	which serves the best coffee in the city.
2	That's the café	a	b	where Shakespeare was born.
3	That's the woman	c	c	whose husband helped us when our car broke down.
4	Athens is	e	d	which she bought last month.
5	I remember the time	h	e	where the Acropolis is.
6	That's the house	b	f	who's wearing the red coat is Lily.
7	The little girl	f	g	who works for Prada.
8	That's the ring	d	h	when my dad first took me to a football match.

4 **Match the beginnings of the sentences (1–8) with their endings (a–h). Write a suitable relative pronoun.**

1	This is the university	b	a	*who / that* flew in space.
2	Valentina Tereshkova was the first woman	a	b	*where* your uncle studied.
3	The shop assistant	f	c	*who / that* I used to work with.
4	Coco Chanel,	h	d	*which / that* I read this morning was very interesting.
5	We met a boy	e	e	*whose* name was Alexander.
6	That's the place	g	f	*who / that* sold me this jacket was really friendly.
7	The magazine article	d	g	*where* Emma bought her wedding dress.
8	They are the people	c	h	*whose* designs made women's fashion more comfortable, was French.

5 Rewrite the sentences using relative pronouns. Use commas where necessary. Then tick the sentences where the relative pronouns can be omitted.

1 Those are the earrings. My friend gave them to me. ✓

 Those are the earrings which / that my friend gave to me.

2 This is the girl. Her cousin works as a model. ☐

 This is the girl whose cousin works as a model.

3 This is the boy. He's my brother's friend from college. ☐

 This is the boy who / that is my brother's friend from college.

4 They work in a factory. The factory makes gloves. ☐

 They work in a factory which / that makes gloves.

5 We'll meet on Saturday. We can talk about your party. ☐

 We'll meet on Saturday when we can talk about your party.

6 That's the designer. She won an award last month. ☐

 That's the designer who / that won an award last month.

7 That's the cinema. I saw a film there on Saturday. ☐

 That's the cinema where I saw a film on Saturday.

8 This is the car. We got it last year. ✓

 This is the car which / that we got last year.

6 Complete the sentences in two different ways.

1 Siya is playing with a girl. The girl is her sister.

 a The girl *who Siya is playing with is her sister.*

 b The girl *Siya is playing with is her sister.*

2 He works with a marine biologist. The marine biologist is very well known.

 a The marine biologist *who / that he works with is very well known.*

 b The marine biologist *he works with is very well known.*

3 We borrowed some blankets from our friends. The blankets were made of wool.

 a The blankets *which / that we borrowed from our friends were made of wool.*

 b The blankets *we borrowed from our friends were made of wool.*

4 Karl has gone to a fashion show. The fashion show is in Paris.

 a The fashion show *which / that Karl has gone to is in Paris.*

 b The fashion show *Karl has gone to is in Paris.*

5 He was talking to a man. The man is his English teacher.

 a The man *who / that he was talking to is his English teacher.*

 b The man *he was talking to is his English teacher.*

6 We went for a run during the day. The day was sunny and hot.

 a The day *when we went for a run was sunny and hot.*

 b The day *we went for a run was sunny and hot.*

Sentence transformation

7 Complete the second sentence so that it has a similar meaning to the first sentence, using the word given. Do not change the word given. You must use between two and five words.

1 My mother was born in 1971.
   1971 _____*was the year when*_____ my mother was born.   **WHEN**

2 Both of his brothers are vegetarian.
   He's _____*got two brothers who*_____ are vegetarian.   **WHO**

3 I borrowed an umbrella from that girl.
   She _____*'s / is the girl whose umbrella*_____ I borrowed.   **WHOSE**

4 Their cousin shops online all evening.
   They've _____*got a cousin that*_____ shops online all evening.   **THAT**

5 I repaired my blouse at the weekend.
   This _____*is the blouse which*_____ I repaired at the weekend.   **WHICH**

6 When we went on holiday, we stayed at the Sunny Hotel in Rome.
   It was the Sunny Hotel in Rome _____*where we stayed*_____ on holiday.   **WHERE**

7 All visitors to the tennis club need to bring their own equipment.
   Everyone _____*who visits the tennis club*_____ needs to bring their own equipment.   **VISITS**

8 I found these glasses on the street.
   These _____*are the glasses that*_____ I found on the street.   **THAT**

Vocabulary

Word formation

8 Choose the correct option to complete the sentences.

1 He never wants to (disappoint) / disappointment / disappointed his parents.
2 They've decorated the rooms of their house really elegance / (elegantly) / elegant.
3 The originate / (origin) / original of the word 'fashionable' is from one of Shakespeare's plays.
4 She's well-prepared for her interview, which will hopefully (impress) / impressed / impression everyone.
5 The lawyers worked very profession / professional / (professionally), but they didn't enjoy the job.
6 Why don't you leave an advertise / (advert) / advertising on the school website for your second-hand books?
7 There was so much confuse / confused / (confusion) in the shop when the lights went off!
8 The clothes you choose to wear can be an express / expressive / (expression) of your personality.

9 Use the word in capitals to form a word that fits in the gap.

1 Our aunt makes clothes as a hobby, but they look really _____*professional*_____ .   **PROFESSION**
2 He bought an _____*elegant*_____ suit for the wedding.   **ELEGANCE**
3 She's the model who appeared in the _____*advertising*_____ campaigns.   **ADVERTISE**
4 My dad gets _____*confused*_____ when he shops online.   **CONFUSE**
5 Whenever she needs to _____*express*_____ her feelings, she talks to her sister.   **EXPRESSION**
6 They weren't _____*impressed*_____ with the meal, which was cold and tasteless.   **IMPRESSION**
7 I was _____*disappointed*_____ when they closed down the department store.   **DISAPPOINTMENT**
8 He doesn't follow fashion and prefers to wear _____*original*_____ clothes.   **ORIGIN**

7

Exam practice

Multiple-choice cloze

10 **For each question, choose the correct answer.**

1 She bought herself an expensive ___ bag when she got her new job.
- **A** cotton
- **B** glass
- **C** leather
- **D** metal

2 The item of ___ I wear the most is my black T-shirt.
- **A** clothing
- **B** cloth
- **C** clothes
- **D** clothe

3 His designer suit was very elegant – the handkerchief pocket even had a blue ___ lining!
- **A** silver
- **B** plastic
- **C** wool
- **D** silk

4 My parents prefer to buy ___ clothes that last longer than fast fashion.
- **A** well-paid
- **B** well-made
- **C** well-dressed
- **D** well-prepared

5 He wasn't very excited ___ the idea of having a large shopping mall in town.
- **A** about
- **B** in
- **C** to
- **D** for

6 Make sure you read the washing instructions on the ___ .
- **A** receipt
- **B** ticket
- **C** label
- **D** note

7 I don't like shopping online – I never know where to look and I soon ___ interest.
- **A** go
- **B** lose
- **C** get
- **D** drop

8 Why don't we have a clothes ___ party so we can get some different clothes without buying any?
- **A** change
- **B** repair
- **C** fit
- **D** swap

Open cloze

11 **For each question, write the correct answer. Write one word for each gap.**

1 On Fridays we can wear __*casual*__ clothes in the office – we don't need to be smart.

2 That's the boy __*whose*__ parents recently split up.

3 I much prefer wearing a __*pair*__ of trousers to a dress or a skirt.

4 That's the outdoor market __*where*__ I bought some delicious fruit.

5 Small independent shops, __*which*__ I think are really important, need a lot of regular customers.

6 Do you remember the day __*when*__ we first met?

7 Why don't you put on something more brightly __*coloured*__ ? You always wear black!

8 My brother, __*who*__ works as a gardener, lives in Oxford.

Speaking

12 **Work in pairs. Discuss these things with your partner.**

- a place where you enjoy going with your friends
- a special day that you have never forgotten about
- the clothes that you like and don't like to wear
- a person whose style of clothes you like

1 Which of these sentences are correct (C) and incorrect (I)?

1 When she gets home she'll play with you. __I__

2 I'll do the washing up before I go to bed. __C__

3 He'll email you after he will get to the hotel. __I__

4 You can't have any ice cream until you've eaten your dinner. __C__

5 After Grandma and Grandpa arrived, we'll go into the garden. __I__

6 The moment your brother finishes his homework, it'll be time for bed. __C__

7 Before they came, they'll call. __I__

8 Will you help me with these boxes after you have eaten? __C__

9 I'll fix your bike when I've fixed mine. __C__

10 I'll change my clothes as soon I'll get home. __I__

How many did you get right? ☐

Grammar

Clauses with time expressions

When we use time expressions such as *when, before, after, until, the moment, as soon as,* etc. to talk about the future, we follow them with a present or a present perfect tense. We do not use them with a future tense.

***After** we **finish** our project, we'll help you with your homework.*

***The moment** Kevin **gets** home, I'll ask him to call you.*

We use a present perfect tense to emphasise that the first action is finished before the other one starts. We cannot use a present tense if one action has finished.

*You can go out and play **when** you've **tidied** your room.* (You'll tidy your room first and then you'll go out and play.)

***When** everyone **has taken** a seat, we'll get started.* (Everyone will take a seat first and then we'll start.)

Grammar exercises

2 Choose the correct option to complete the sentences.

1 I won't stop *after / until* I've fixed this car!

2 *As soon as / Until* Joe arrives in London, he'll visit Big Ben.

3 He'll call us *until / after* he finishes his driving test.

4 They'll cut the grass *after / before* it starts raining.

5 Dean will call us *until / when* he gets home.

6 I'll read you a story as *soon as / until* you fall asleep.

7 Will you buy a new phone *as soon as / before* you've saved enough money?

8 You can't play computer games *the moment / before* you've studied for the test.

8

3 Rewrite the sentences adding commas where necessary. Tick those which do not need a comma.

1 My sister will look after you until your parents get home.
✓

2 Before I go out I'll help you with your homework.
Before I go out, I'll help you with your homework.

3 The moment I find my phone I'll give her a ring.
The moment I find my phone, I'll give her a ring.

4 We'll visit our grandparents when we go to Surrey.
✓

5 Before you leave I'll make you a few sandwiches.
Before you leave, I'll make you a few sandwiches.

6 I'll buy you a treat after we've finished doing the shopping.
✓

7 As soon as I know what we're doing I'll text him.
As soon as I know what we're doing, I'll text him.

8 He'll ask her to marry him after he's found a good job.
✓

9 They'll buy a new house as soon as they've saved some money.
✓

10 After your parents leave we'll decorate the house for the party.
After your parents leave, we'll decorate the house for the party.

4 Underline the action which is finished before the other starts.

1 You can have some new jeans when you've worn out your old jeans.
2 As soon as I've saved €50, I'll buy those shoes.
3 We'll leave for the shops as soon as Megan has arrived.
4 You can't return the jumper until you've found the receipt.
5 I'll choose one t-shirt after I've tried them all on.
6 When the shops have closed, we'll get something to eat.
7 She can't go into the changing room until the person in there has come out.
8 After he's paid for those gloves, he can put them on and get warm.

5 Complete the sentences with *before*, *after*, *until*, or *as soon as*. Use each time expression twice.

1 _____After_____ I finish my high school exams, I'll go to university.
2 _____Before_____ he goes to the party, he'll dress up in some smart clothes.
3 _As soon as_ I find your bracelet, I'll text you.
4 I'll go into a changing room _as soon as_ there is one free.
5 I'll save some money for shoes _____after_____ I buy the dress.
6 You can wear my scarf _____until_____ we get home.
7 I'll pick up all the clothes off the floor _____before_____ I leave the house.
8 _____Until_____ you get a new watch, I'll lend you mine.

6 Circle the correct time expression and complete the sentences with the present simple or future simple (*will*) form of the verbs.

1 I'll send you a letter *before* / *the moment* I ____arrive____ (arrive) in France.
2 You can come and stay with me *when* / *before* I ____buy____ (buy) my own flat.
3 We ____'ll go____ (go) for a walk *before* / *after* it has stopped raining.
4 *When* / *Before* she ____reads____ (read) the recipe, she'll know how to make the cake.
5 I can't do the ironing *after* / *until* I ____wash____ (wash) the clothes!
6 We ____won't leave____ (not leave) for the airport *until* / *when* she finds her passport!
7 The students won't know the results *after* / *until* they ____'re____ (be) on the notice board.
8 *As soon as* / *Before* I get in the house, I ____'ll change____ (change) into something cooler.

7 Complete the sentences with the present simple or future simple (*will*) form of the verbs.

1 The doctor ____will contact____ (contact) you as soon as he ____has____ (have) your results.
2 The moment the train ____gets____ (get) into the station, I ____'ll board____ (board) it.
3 They ____won't move____ (not move) house until their children ____finish____ (finish) school.
4 After John ____returns____ (return), we ____'ll decide____ (decide) what to order for dinner.
5 The moment we ____open____ (open) the gate, the dog ____will jump____ (jump) on us!
6 When you ____complete____ (complete) the form, I ____'ll come____ (come) and collect it.
7 Mum and Dad ____will miss____ (miss) me after I ____leave____ (leave) for university.
8 He ____'ll tell____ (tell) Brett about the party the moment he ____sees____ (see) him.
9 I ____'ll give____ (give) you the tablet as soon as I ____take____ (take) a look at the news.
10 She ____'ll go____ (go) to bed after she ____reads____ (read) one more chapter.

Vocabulary

Phrasal verbs

8 Complete the definitions with these words. You will need to use some words more than once.

at	around	for	on	out	up	with

1 When you find something ____out____ , you get new information.
2 When two things look good together, they go ____with____ each other.
3 When you look ____at____ something, you use your eyes to examine it.
4 When you pay ____for____ something, you use your money to buy it.
5 When you pick something ____up____ , you use your hands to take and hold it.
6 When you shop ____around____ , you look at the prices in different shops before you buy.
7 When you try clothes ____on____ , you wear them because you want to know if they fit and look good.
8 When your shoes wear ____out____ , they have become too old and you can't use them anymore.

9 Complete the sentences with the correct form of the phrasal verbs from Exercise 8.

1 The woman in the shop said I mustn't ____try____ the glasses ____on____ because I might break them.
2 She spoke to the shop assistant because she wanted to ____find out____ where the changing rooms were.
3 I always ____shop around____ when I buy things online because prices are different from different sellers.
4 I loved the dress, but when I ____put____ it ____on____ , it was very loose.
5 He really wanted the coat, but when he looked ____looked at____ the price on the label, he couldn't buy it.
6 If you buy good quality clothes, they don't ____wear out____ quickly.
7 Does this scarf ____go with____ my jacket?
8 Her parents ____pay for____ all of her things, so she doesn't have to get a part-time job.

8

Exam practice

Multiple-choice cloze

10 Choose the correct answers.

1 She always ___ sunglasses, even at night!

   A puts   **B** wears   **C** has   **D** tries

2 The second-hand designer dress was an amazing ___ – only £2!

   A bargain   **B** sale   **C** prize   **D** cost

3 Some people like to wear tight clothes to exercise in, but I prefer something ___ .

   A free   **B** easy   **C** relaxing   **D** loose

4 When you want to look ___ , just put on a black jacket.

   A bright   **B** suitable   **C** smart   **D** appropriate

5 The necklace was made in the 1920s. It's ___ , but it is fashionable, today.

   A old-fashioned   **B** antique   **C** original   **D** classical

6 Don't forget to get a ___ for your jeans because you might want to return them.

   A receipt   **B** recipe   **C** record   **D** reading

7 I thought the woman was a shop assistant, but she was just a ___ like me.

   A buyer   **B** worker   **C** customer   **D** employer

8 You need to pay with ___ here – they don't take credit cards.

   A change   **B** coin   **C** money   **D** cash

Open cloze

11 For each question, write the correct answer. Write one word for each gap.

1 We didn't leave the restaurant __until__ it was very dark outside.

2 I thought I was lost, but __then__ I saw my friend.

3 The driver said he'd __pay__ for the damage to my bicycle.

4 The birds fly south as __soon__ as the winter arrives.

5 Unfortunately, her jacket didn't __go__ with her skirt.

6 I was worried about the price __at__ first, but it wasn't expensive.

7 He stopped and __looked__ at every painting in the museum.

8 The fashion show started __the__ moment I found my seat.

Writing

12 Read the writing task and write a short story in about 100 words. Try to use sequencing words and adjectives to describe feelings and places.

Write a short story beginning with this sentence:
Alex saw the clothes on the bedroom chair and knew the big day had arrived!

Grammar

1 **Choose the correct option to complete the sentences.**

1 We _have destroyed_ / _destroyed_ many plant and animal species in the last 50 years.

2 Over the decades, climate change _caused_ / _has caused_ seas to become warmer and glaciers to melt.

3 The marine biologist _returned_ / _has returned_ from her research centre in Australia a week ago.

4 I _have seen_ / _saw_ elephants and lions when I visited Kenya.

5 A team of researchers _studied_ / _has been studying_ the effects of pollution for years now.

6 In 2019, the politician _has fought_ / _fought_ plans to build a new power plant.

7 The use of renewable energy _has reduced_ / _reduced_ our use of fossil fuels in the past few years.

8 What _has your son been doing_ / _did your son do_ since he finished university?

9 We _bought_ / _have been buying_ our clothes in second-hand shops recently.

10 So far this month, she _sold_ / _has sold_ more than half her products in independent shops.

2 **Complete the sentences with _a_, _an_, _the_ or – (no article).**

1 We need to do something to help _____the_____ environment before it's too late.

2 Can you understand why _____–_____ people aren't interested in being eco-friendly?

3 My doctor advised me to eat something light for _____–_____ lunch each day.

4 My cousin is _____an_____ explorer; she's been to some interesting places.

5 There's a monkey in the tree. _____The_____ monkey is eating some fruit.

6 Do you know the location of _____the_____ Galápagos Islands?

7 Their uncle speaks many languages; he even speaks _____–_____ Hawaiian.

8 My dad said we're going on holiday to _____the_____ Alps; I'm so excited about seeing some snow!

9 Have you ever seen _____a_____ shark in the wild?

10 I don't like travelling by _____–_____ plane; let's take the train instead.

3 **Choose the correct option (a–b) to complete the sentences.**

1 In some states in the USA, turning sixteen is a time ___ you can drive a car.
   a that
   b when

2 My cousin, ___ mother is a biologist, really cares about the planet.
   a whose
   b who his

3 That's the building ___ they're doing research on the effects of climate change.
   a where
   b which

4 This is the café ___ I met my best friend.
   a that
   b where

5 My grandad, ___ I am named after, is a very kind person.
   a who
   b that

6 The cat ___ comes into our garden all the time is black and white.
   a that
   b who

7 In the autumn, ___ the leaves on the trees change colour, we like going for walks.
   a who
   b when

8 The article, ___ is about Costa Rica, is worth reading.
   a that
   b which

4 **Find the mistake and write A or B in the box. Then correct the mistakes.**

1 As soon as you'll (A) get home, dinner will be (B) ready. [A]

   As soon as you get home, dinner will be ready.

2 Before she visits (A) the Greek island, she books (B) a hotel room. [B]

   Before she visits the Greek island, she'll book a hotel room.

3 When I'll finish (A) my project, I'll go out (B) with my friends. [A]

   When I finish my project, I'll go out with my friends.

4 Susie moves (A) to New Zealand when she finishes (B) university. [A]

   Susie will move to New Zealand when she finishes university.

5 After I've finished (A) making the invitations, I send (B) them. [B]

   After I've finished making the invitations, I'll send them.

6 They watched (A) TV as soon as they've had (B) lunch. [A]

   They'll watch TV as soon as they've had lunch.

7 Don't worry. He'll email (A) you the moment he'll arrive (B) in Brazil. [B]

   Don't worry. He'll email you the moment he arrives in Brazil.

8 Kevin will play (A) computer games until he has done (B) the washing-up. [A]

   Kevin won't play computer games until he has done the washing-up.

9 Nina will buy (A) a present before she went (B) to the party. [B]

   Nina will buy a present before she goes to the party.

10 My parents will buy (A) a smaller house after my brother and I'll leave (B) home. [B]

   My parents will a buy smaller house after my brother and I leave / have left home.

5 **Find one mistake in each sentence. Then correct the mistakes.**

1 The Dodo bird was extinct for over 300 years now.

   The Dodo bird has been extinct for over 300 years now.

2 I always close the windows after I leave the house.

   I always close the windows before I leave the house.

3 Tina is only twenty, but she's already gone to Europe, Asia and South America.

   Tina is only twenty, but she's already been to Europe, Asia and South America.

4 My best friend, that is an amazing student, always helps me with maths.

   My best friend, who is an amazing student, always helps me with maths.

5 Those scientists have travelled to the Easter Island.

   Those scientists have travelled to Easter Island.

6 We'll never forget the time which we saw a bear.

   We'll never forget the time when we saw a bear.

7 Our dog has dug in the garden for ages.

   Our dog has been digging in the garden for ages.

8 I've been waiting since an hour now; where are you?

   I've been waiting for an hour now; where are you?

6 Choose the correct option to complete the sentences.

1 We've been studying marine life at school *since* / *for* March.
2 Can your brother play *the* / *a* drums?
3 The platypus, *that* / *which* is a strange animal, lives in Australia.
4 Cars and planes *have been producing* / *produced* air pollution for decades.
5 When I grow up, I *will work* / *have worked* for NASA.
6 The scientist *has discovered* / *discovered* a new species of spider last month.
7 I'm going to – / *the* school on Elm Street to play football.
8 My mother, *who* / *whose* teaches English, speaks French too.
9 Julia *has been* / *has gone* to the library; she'll be back soon.
10 You can't have dessert *as soon as* / *until* you've eaten your vegetables.

Use of English

Open cloze

7 For each question, write the correct answer. Write one word for each gap.

1 When we get to the station, we ____will____ give you a call.
2 The explorer has been in Antarctica ____since____ 2020.
3 I tried ____on____ a lovely pair of leather boots, but they didn't fit.
4 My parents and I have ____been____ to many countries in Europe.
5 He can't go to the cinema; he hasn't finished his homework ____yet____ .
6 He turned part of his garden ____into____ a vegetable patch.
7 I don't think those earrings go ____with____ your blouse. The colours aren't right.
8 Have you ____ever____ met anyone famous?
9 ____How____ long has your brother been studying butterflies?
10 Let me pay ____for____ your dinner as a thank you for all your advice.

Word formation

8 Use the word in capitals to form a word that fits in the gap.

1 For polar bears to ____survive____ , we need to stop glaciers from melting.   **SURVIVAL**
2 The Great Wall of China is ____visible____ from space.   **VISION**
3 Sources of energy that are ____renewable____ include wind and solar power.   **RENEW**
4 You can put your food waste in ____biodegradable____ bags.   **BIODEGRADE**
5 I'm really ____confused____ – I don't understand these instructions at all!   **CONFUSE**
6 In the past, we used to watch a lot of ____adverts____ on TV, but now we don't need to.   **ADVERTISE**
7 My parents weren't ____impressed____ with my sister's school report.   **IMPRESS**
8 He baked a cake for his nephew's birthday, but he was a bit ____disappointed____ with the result.   **DISAPPOINT**

Grammar

9 For questions 1–10, choose the word or phrase that best completes the sentence.

1 Is that the place ___ the orangutans live?
   A when
   B which
   C where
   D that

2 Have you been a researcher ___ a long time?
   A since
   B for
   C yet
   D already

3 Look at ___ moon – it's huge!
   A an
   B a
   C the
   D –

4 They ___ on a trip to Brazil last year.
   A go
   B have been
   C have gone
   D went

5 ___ Dad gets home, he'll fix your bike.
   A When
   B Until
   C Before
   D Soon

6 We ___ round in this cave for hours!
   A walked
   B have walked
   C have been walking
   D are walking

7 Ben, ___ is twenty, is my best friend.
   A who
   B that
   C whose
   D where

8 As soon as I get to the office, I ___ the doctor.
   A have emailed
   B emailed
   C will be emailing
   D will email

9 Biology, ___ is a subject I study, is great.
   A that
   B which
   C who
   D whose

10 My grandmother is in ___ hospital.
   A –
   B an
   C the
   D a

Vocabulary

10 For questions 11–20, choose the word or phrase that best completes the sentence.

11 She wants to ___ up a sports club.
   A get
   B set
   C bring
   D give

12 Over the edge of the ___ , I saw the ocean.
   A cave
   B river
   C cliff
   D valley

13 The team managed to clean ___ three beaches.
   A up
   B with
   C in
   D round

14 He wears ___ clothes from the 1950s.
   A casual
   B loose
   C vintage
   D tight

15 I've just found this jacket. What a ___ !
   A show
   B label
   C receipt
   D bargain

16 Cycling is a good way to ___ pollution.
   A reduce
   B remove
   C survive
   D collect

17 Let's take ___ to reduce rubbish on our streets.
   A time
   B part
   C action
   D place

18 Every time I start learning a new language, I quickly ___ interest and stop.
   A find
   B lose
   C get
   D make

19 I'm ___ about going to the concert.
   A excitement
   B excite
   C excitingly
   D excited

20 We sell everything ___ matches to ice.
   A for
   B from
   C with
   D at

Unit 9

1 Which of these sentences are correct (C) and incorrect (I)?

1 It's suddenly got cold. I'm going to get my jacket. ___I___

2 They're going to move house at the weekend. ___C___

3 My boyfriend will be a famous actor some day! ___C___

4 Sally isn't going to do that again. She promised. ___I___

5 Stop making noise or I'll tell Mum. ___C___

6 My grandmother is going to be 70 years old next Wednesday. ___I___

7 Maybe we'll visit the Empire State Building when we're in New York City. ___C___

8 Wait, I'll help you move that table. ___C___

9 Are you going to take the rubbish out, please? ___I___

10 Look! That little boy will burn himself on the cooker. ___I___

How many did you get right? ☐

Grammar

will

Affirmative	Negative	Questions
I / He / She / It / We / You / They **will** clean.	I / He / She / It / We / You / They **will not** (**won't**) clean.	**Will** I / he / she / it / we / you / they clean?
Short Answers		
Yes, I / he / she / it **will**. **Yes**, we / you / they **will**.	**No**, I / he / she / it **won't**. **No**, we / you / they **won't**.	

We use *will*:
- for decisions made at the time of speaking.
I'll ask my dad to take us to school.
- for predictions.
Scotland will win the match.
- for promises.
We won't make a mess again. We promise.
- for threats.
If you tell anyone, I'll never speak to you again!
- to talk about future facts.
Karen will be 15 years old next week.
- after verbs like *think, believe, be sure, expect*, etc. and words like *probably, maybe*, etc.
We expect they'll share a flat when they move to the city.
- to offer to do something for someone.
I will help you do the washing up.
- to ask someone to do something.
Will you tidy up your room, please?

be going to

Affirmative	Negative	Questions
I **am** ('**m**) **going to** clean. He / She / It **is** ('**s**) **going to** clean. We / You / They **are** ('**re**) **going to** clean.	I **am** ('**m**) **not going to** clean. He / She / It **is not** (**isn't**) **going to** clean. We / You / They **are not** (**aren't**) **going to** clean.	**Am** I **going to** clean? **Is** he / she / it **going to** clean? **Are** we / you / they **going to** clean?

Short Answers		
Yes, I **am**. **Yes**, we / you / they **are**. **Yes**, he / she / it **is**.	**No**, I'm **not**. **No**, we / you / they **aren't**. **No**, he / she / it **isn't**.	

We use *be going to* for:
- future plans.

We're going to decorate our bedroom at the weekend.

- predictions for the near future based on present situations or evidence.

*Oh no! That paint is wet and Billy **is going to** get it all over his trousers.*

> **Note**
>
> We often use these common time expressions with *will* and *be going to*: *this week / month / summer, tonight, this evening, tomorrow, tomorrow morning / afternoon / night, next week / month / year, at the weekend, in January, in a few minutes / hours / days, on Thursday, on Wednesday morning*, etc.
>
> *He's going to move house **next week**.*

Grammar exercises

2 **Choose the correct use of *will* (a–b).**

1 We'll go to the market for you, Mum.
  - (a) to offer to do something for someone
  - b to talk about future facts

2 My children will design their own houses one day.
  - a for threats
  - (b) for predictions without having any evidence

3 Will you please clean the kitchen for me?
  - (a) to ask someone to do something
  - b after certain verbs

4 He won't make a mess in the living room. He said so.
  - a for decisions made at the time of speaking
  - (b) for promises

5 Don't shout at me or I'll make you go to your room!
  - (a) for threats
  - b for predictions without having any evidence

6 I'll get my coat and meet you at the library.
  - (a) for decisions made at the time of speaking
  - b to ask someone to do something

7 Sofia will be five years old next week.
  - a for promises
  - (b) to talk about future facts

8 She believes she'll find a cheap flat in the city centre.
  - a to offer to do something for someone
  - (b) after certain verbs

3 Use the prompts to write questions with *will*. Then complete the short answers.

1 he / have a party on his birthday this year?
   A: *Will he have a party on his birthday this year?*   **B:** No, *he won't* .

2 you / eat fast food on Saturday night?
   A: *Will you eat fast food on Saturday night?*   **B:** Yes, *I will* .

3 she / start work when she finishes school?
   A: *Will she start work when she finishes school?*   **B:** No, *she won't* .

4 they / travel to Melbourne next winter?
   A: *Will they travel to Melbourne next winter?*   **B:** No, *they won't* .

5 we / move house in the future?
   A: *Will we move house in the future?*   **B:** Yes, *we will* .

6 you / be an architect when you grow up?
   A: *Will you be an architect when you grow up?*   **B:** No, *I won't* .

7 Tom and Mia / buy a bungalow when they're retired?
   A: *Will Tom and Mia buy a bungalow when they're retired?*   **B:** Yes, *they will* .

8 Jake / plant a garden at his cottage in the summer?
   A: *Will Jake plant a garden at his cottage in the summer?*   **B:** Yes, *he will* .

4 Complete the sentences so that they are true for you. Use *will* and *I think, I believe, I am sure, I expect, I hope, I doubt,* and the words *probably* and *maybe.* *Students' own answers*

1 What will you have for lunch today?

2 Who will you live with when you're an adult?

3 Where will you be at seven o'clock tomorrow evening?

4 When will you move out of your parents' house?

5 What kind of house will you live in when you're older?

6 Where will you go on holiday this summer?

7 When will you next visit relatives?

8 What will you get for your next birthday?

5 **What will the future be like? Use the prompts and *will* to write sentences.**

1 robots and machines / do all the work in factories ✓
  Robots and machines will do all the work in factories.

2 people / travel to work and school by flying cars ✗
  People won't travel to work and school by flying cars.

3 pollution / get worse and worse ✓
  Pollution will get worse and worse.

4 families / go on holiday to other planets ✗
  Families won't go on holiday to other planets.

5 people / live in huge skyscrapers ✓
  People will live in huge skyscrapers.

6 children / stop learning other languages ✗
  Children won't stop learning other languages.

7 people / be healthier and have longer lives ✓
  People will be healthier and have longer lives.

8 animals / only live in zoos ✗
  Animals won't only live in zoos.

6 **Kate and her family are planning to go on holiday this winter. Write the words in order to make questions about their future plans. Then complete the short answers.**

1 fly / to / going to / are / their destination / Kate and her family
  A: *Are Kate and her family going to fly to their destination?*   B: No, *they aren't* .

2 a cottage / going to / are / rent / Kate and her family
  A: *Are Kate and her family going to rent a cottage?*   B: No, *they aren't* .

3 going to / Kate and her brother / a castle / visit / are
  A: *Are Kate and her brother going to visit a castle?*   B: Yes, *they are* .

4 Kate's brother / visit friends / is / going to
  A: *Is Kate's brother going to visit friends?*   B: Yes, *he is* .

5 going to / are / in restaurants / eat out / Kate and her family
  A: *Are Kate and her family going to eat out in restaurants?*   B: Yes, *they are* .

6 swim / are / in the sea / going to / Kate and her brother
  A: *Are Kate and her brother going to swim in the sea?*   B: No, *they aren't* .

7 climb / going to / Kate's mother / a mountain / is
  A: *Is Kate's mother going to climb a mountain?*   B: No, *she isn't* .

8 going to / lots of photos / is / take / Kate
  A: *Is Kate going to take lots of photos?*   B: Yes, *she is* .

7 Complete the conversations with the correct form of *will* or *be going to* and the verbs.

1 **A:** I've finally decided what to put in the new living room.
  B: Really? What _____*are you going to put*_____ (you / put) in there?

2 **A:** Look! It's started to rain.
  B: Oh, _____*will you close*_____ (you / close) all the windows, please?

3 **A:** Do you know your schedule for next week?
  B: Yes. We _____*'re going to work*_____ (work) on a new building project.

4 **A:** Sammy, look what you've done to your room! What a mess!
  B: I'm sorry, Mum. I promise I _____*won't do*_____ (not / do) that again.

5 **A:** Look at that man putting a watch in his pocket.
  B: Oh no. He _____*'s going to steal*_____ (steal) it!

6 **A:** Have you finished decorating your new chest of drawers yet?
  B: No, but I'm sure I _____*'ll finish*_____ (finish) it very soon.

7 **A:** Did you empty the dishwasher for me?
  B: No, we forgot. We _____*'ll empty*_____ (empty) it right now!

8 **A:** How old is your brother?
  B: Theo _____*will be*_____ (be) sixteen next Sunday.

Vocabulary

Prepositions

8 Complete the phrases with these prepositions.

around	at	for	from	in	on (x2)	to (x2)	with

1 get electricity __*from*__ wind power
2 stay __*for*__ a week
3 move from one place __*to*__ another
4 get on __*with*__ everyone
5 wrap a blanket __*around*__ you
6 live __*on*__ the second floor
7 be close __*to*__ the beach
8 live __*on*__ your own
9 __*in*__ the past
10 __*at*__ the end of

9 Complete the sentences with the correct prepositions from Exercise 8.

1 I didn't get on __*with*__ my new flatmate – he was annoying.
2 She gets all her vintage clothes __*from*__ the second-hand shop.
3 The little boy was cold, so I wrapped my scarf __*around*__ him.
4 He shared a house with friends because he didn't want to live __*on*__ his own.
5 My parents stayed in a bungalow that was close __*to*__ a farm.
6 They've rented a flat __*on*__ the sixth floor.
7 My sister is starting university __*at*__ the end of September.
8 Do you think more people will live in rented property __*in*__ the future?
9 We moved from the city __*to*__ the countryside to escape the pollution.
10 My parents stayed in Abu Dhabi __*for*__ the weekend and then went to Dubai.

9

Exam practice

Open cloze

10 **For each question, write the correct answer. Write one word for each gap.**

1 I doubt they ____will____ work today – it's Saturday!
2 If you make a mess, Mum will ____not____ let you watch TV.
3 My uncle has promised he ____will____ take us to the design show.
4 ____Are____ you going to be home later this evening?
5 They've got a plan. They're ____going____ to build the tallest skyscraper in the world.
6 We aren't going ____to____ move into a flat; my husband doesn't like them.
7 Oh no! That little girl's toy ____is____ going to fall down the stairs.
8 My brother will ____be____ nineteen next month.

Multiple-choice cloze

11 **For each question, choose the correct answer.**

1 When we've finished dinner, can you wash up and put the dishes ___ ?
   A in   B out   C round   **D** away
2 My sister is going to move into an apartment ___ .
   A square   **B** block   C building   D property
3 Students sometimes pay high ___ for bad accommodation.
   A salaries   **B** rents   C refunds   D receipts
4 The king lived in a huge stone ___ at the very top of a mountain.
   A castle   B bungalow   C flat   D houseboat
5 The problem with our cottage is that the windows are small and the ___ are low.
   A ceilings   B balconies   C floors   D walls
6 I'll put the plates in the ___ now.
   A fridge   **B** dishwasher   C washing machine   D freezer
7 If you pass me the ___ , I'll make us a cup of tea.
   A kettle   B brush   C ladder   D iron
8 He'll have a ___ when he finishes in the garden – he'll be dirty.
   A seat   B soap   **C** shower   D lunch

Speaking

12 **Work in pairs. Discuss the questions.**

- What kind of house will you live in when you leave your family home?
- How will you pay the rent?
- Do you think you'll live in the city or the countryside?
- Have you decided what kind of place you are going to live in?
- Have you planned how you are going to decorate your place?
- Do you think you'll share your new place with anyone else?

Unit 10

1 Which of these sentences are correct (C) and incorrect (I)?

1 When she retires, she's going to travel to India. _C_

2 They're sure they might pass their exams. _I_

3 Sorry, I'll be busy tomorrow – my aunt is visiting for the day. _I_

4 Have you eaten that whole bar of chocolate? You're going to be ill. _C_

5 Her brother isn't going to move away from home – he loves being with his family. _C_

6 The train is going to leave at eight o'clock. _I_

7 We may go to the shopping mall later, but we haven't decided yet. _C_

8 Watch out for that kite – it's out of control and it'll hit someone! _I_

9 Ticket sales end at midnight on Wednesday 10th May. _C_

10 He might to apply for the interior design course. _I_

How many did you get right? ☐

Grammar

Future plans and events

- We use *be going to* for future plans and intentions when we haven't made any definite arrangements yet.
When I've finished college, I'm going to do a creative writing course.
- We use the present continuous for future plans when fixed arrangements have been made. We usually use a time expression the first time the plan is mentioned.
This weekend we're seeing some friends who we met on holiday. We're having a barbecue at their house.
- We use the present simple for future events that are on a timetable or follow a schedule. We usually give the time or date of the event.
The outdoor cinema opens on 1st June and closes on 15th September.

Future predictions

- We use *be going to* for future predictions when there is evidence in the present situation, especially something we can see or hear.
Your music is much too loud. You're going to damage your ears.
- We use *will* for future predictions about what we think will happen, often based on our opinions or on past experience.
I know he'll buy her an expensive birthday present – he's very generous.
- We use *may* or *might* to talk about a future possibility – we aren't sure it will happen.
Kat may paint her bedroom blue, or she may paint it green.
She might buy a new bed.

> **Note**
>
> We use *may* and *might* + infinitive without *to*.
> *We may move house next year, but it depends on my mum's job.*

10

Grammar exercises

2 Use the prompts to write sentences about future plans and intentions.

1 when / he / older, / he / snorkel / in the Galápagos Islands ✓
   When he's older, he's going to snorkel in the Galápagos Islands.

2 after they retire, / they / move to a smaller house ✗
   After they retire, they aren't going to move to a smaller house.

3 before / we / finish college, / we / learn a new sport ✓
   Before we finish college, we're going to learn a new sport.

4 in the future, / she / walk along the Great Wall of China ✓
   In the future, she's going to walk along the Great Wall of China.

5 after / he / work / for a few months, / he / live with his parents anymore ✗
   After he's worked for a few months, he isn't going to live with his parents anymore.

6 when / I / get / my qualifications, / I / study abroad for a year ✓
   When I get my qualifications, I'm going to study abroad for a year.

7 when / they / get enough experience, / they / set up a business ✓
   When they get enough experience, they're going to set up a business.

8 Paul / go / on an expensive holiday when / he / save / some money ✗
   Paul isn't going to go on an expensive holiday when he's saved some money.

9 when / I / fit enough, / I / enter marathon ✓
   When I'm fit enough, I'm going to enter a marathon.

10 after / our / next holiday, / we / travel by plane anymore ✗
   After our next holiday, we aren't going to travel by plane anymore.

3 Use the prompts to write questions using the present continuous. Then complete the short answers.

1 (he / prepare) for the birthday party this morning?
   A: *Is he preparing for the party this morning?*   **B:** No, *he isn't*   .

2 (they / have) dinner with her parents this evening?
   A: *Are they having dinner with her parents this evening?*   **B:** Yes, *they are*   .

3 (your parcel / arrive) today?
   A: *Is your parcel arriving today?*   **B:** Yes, *it is*   .

4 (we / do) the housework after lunch?
   A: *Are we doing the housework after lunch?*   **B:** No, *we aren't*   .

5 (you / move) into your new house next month?
   A: *Are you moving into your new house next month?*   **B:** No, *I'm not*   .

6 (she / work) during the school holidays?
   A: *Is she working during the school holidays?*   **B:** Yes, *she is*   .

4 Use the prompts to write questions and answers with the present simple.

1. what time / plane / arrive / (11.45 a.m.)
   A: _What time does the plane arrive?_
   B: It _arrives at 11.45 a.m._ .

2. when / train / leave / (ten minutes)
   A: _When does the train leave?_
   B: It _leaves in ten minutes_ .

3. they / have got / cooking class this afternoon
   A: _Have they got a cooking class this afternoon?_
   B: Yes, _they have_ .

4. when / show / open / (1st October)
   A: _When does the show open?_
   B: It _opens on 1st October_ .

5. she / have / an English exam next week
   A: _Does she have an English exam next week?_
   B: No, _she doesn't_ .

6. when / the half-price sales / end / (tomorrow)
   A: _When do the half-price sales end?_
   B: They _end tomorrow_ .

7. what time / film / start / (30 minutes)
   A: _What time does the film start?_
   B: It _starts in 30 minutes_ .

8. he / have got / a dentist appointment / this afternoon
   A: _Has he got a dentist appointment this afternoon?_
   B: Yes, _he has_ .

9. when / shopping mall / close / today (nine o'clock)
   A: _When does the shopping mall close today?_
   B: It _closes at nine o'clock_ .

10. she / have got / exciting plans / for the weekend
    A: _Has she got exciting plans for the weekend?_
    B: No, _she hasn't_ .

5 Complete the sentences with *be going to*, the present simple or the present continuous form of the verbs.

1. We _'re renting_ (rent) a cottage by the coast this summer – my mum has just booked it.
2. The show _opens_ (open) in February; I can't wait to see it!
3. In the future, they _'re going to move_ (move) to a warmer climate.
4. He _'s leaving_ (leave) early tomorrow morning because he's got a meeting in Manchester.
5. _Are_ you _doing_ (do) anything this weekend?
6. My uncle _isn't going to retire_ (not / retire); he wants to keep working.
7. She _'s going to start_ (start) running twice a week, so she can get fitter.
8. I _'m seeing_ (see) the doctor at ten o'clock today. I'm not feeling well.

6 **Choose the correct use of the future tenses, (a–b).**

1 We're going build our own house in the future.
  - a for future predictions based on evidence
  - (b) for future plans and intentions

2 The museum closes at six o'clock this evening.
  - (a) for timetabled or scheduled events
  - b for fixed arrangements in the future

3 He might go to university when he finishes school, but he isn't sure.
  - a for future predictions based on evidence
  - (b) for a future possibility

4 Ali knows what Jim is going to choose from the menu – he always has a burger.
  - (a) for future predictions based on opinion or past experience
  - b for fixed arrangements in the future

5 I'm seeing my old flatmate later today.
  - (a) for fixed arrangements in the future
  - b for future predictions based on evidence

6 They may move to the city centre, but it depends on how much it costs.
  - (a) for a future possibility
  - b for timetabled or scheduled events

7 She has a dentist appointment at twelve o'clock.
  - a for future plans or intentions
  - (b) for timetabled or scheduled events

8 That ladder doesn't look safe – he's going to fall.
  - a for future plans and intentions
  - (b) for future predictions based on evidence

7 **Choose the correct option to complete the conversations.**

1 **A:** What do you hope to do when you're older?
  B: I am (going to learn) / learning how to make jewellery.

2 **A:** What are Grant's plans?
  B: He is (flying) / going to fly to Canada tomorrow morning.

3 **A:** What's the weather forecast for the next few days?
  B: (It's going to rain) / It's raining.

4 **A:** Let's ask Julia to come after lunch.
  B: No, she cleans / (is cleaning) her flat this afternoon.

5 **A:** Why are Francis and Diana so excited?
  B: Oh, because they (are moving) / move into their new bungalow tomorrow.

6 **A:** Which room in your house are you going to decorate first?
  B: I (might) / am going to paint the living room first, but I'm not sure.

7 **A:** Do you know the opening times of the furniture shop?
  B: Yes, it is opening / (opens) at 9 a.m. and is closing / (closes) at 5 p.m.

8 **A:** What time are the builders (arriving) / going to arrive?
  B: At seven o'clock in the morning!

9 **A:** Are you (going to tidy up) / tidying up your room sometime soon?
  B: Yes, of course!

10 **A:** How are your neighbours?
  B: They may get married / (are getting married) next year – they've chosen a date in April.

Vocabulary

Collocations and expressions

8 Complete the collocations and expressions using these words.

| be | call | get (x2) | help | make | start | take (x2) | tidy up |

1 _____make_____ your bed
2 _____start_____ your own company
3 _____get_____ access to
4 _____help_____ someone with their homework
5 _____call_____ the police
6 _____take_____ a break
7 _____be_____ half price
8 _____get_____ a job offer
9 _____take_____ a seat
10 _____tidy up_____ the garden

9 Complete the sentences with the correct form of the expressions from Exercise 8.

1 You aren't having breakfast until you've _____made your bed_____ .
2 He hasn't stopped painting all morning; he should _____take a break_____ .
3 My cousin has just _____got a job offer_____ in Italy. She's a fashion designer.
4 He saw a woman steal some earrings, so he _____called the police_____ .
5 All the T-shirts in that shop _____are half price_____ at the moment.
6 When I finish college, I want to _____start my own company_____ , selling hand-made blankets.
7 Many people in the world don't _____get access to_____ electricity or clean running water.
8 Why don't you _____take a seat_____ here while you wait for the others to arrive?
9 My brother is always asking me to _____help him with his homework_____ , but sometimes I don't understand it!
10 They're _____tidying up_____ the garage this weekend – it's a big job.

10

Exam practice

Open cloze

10 For each question, write the correct answer. Write one word for each gap.

1 How ___*about*___ getting a takeaway and watching a film later?

2 The shopping mall ___*opens*___ at 10 a.m. and it doesn't close until midnight.

3 Can you put your clothes away in the ___*chest*___ of drawers?

4 Tom is happy because he ___*is*___ selling his old cottage next week.

5 She may ___*not*___ take the job – she doesn't know if it's right for her.

6 What activities ___*are*___ they doing at the youth club on Tuesday?

7 Please don't ___*make*___ a mess in here – I've just tidied up!

8 I don't think you're ___*going*___ to get a good mobile phone signal here – we're the middle of the countryside.

Multiple-choice cloze

11 For each question, choose the correct answer.

1 The cleaning products are in the cupboard under the ___ sink.
   A living room   B dining room   **C kitchen**   D garden

2 I want to buy some brightly coloured ___ for my sofa.
   A cushions   B curtains   C carpets   D sheets

3 Hang your trousers and dresses in the ___ .
   A shelf   B chair   C bed   **D wardrobe**

4 Did the holiday cottage have ___ access?
   A off-grid   **B internet**   C WiFi   D signal

5 Last winter our ___ stopped working – it was freezing in our house!
   A heat   **B heating**   C heated   D hot

6 The décor of their house is very ___ , but they're going to redecorate soon.
   A old-fashioned   B modern   C sweet   D little

7 He's got a special ___ for his neck.
   A duvet   B blanket   C towel   **D pillow**

8 They want to sell their houseboat so they can live ___ dry land again.
   A in   B for   **C on**   D with

Writing

12 Read the writing task and write your answer in about 100 words. Try to express enthusiasm, and ask for and give information.

You receive an email from your friend telling you about his recent move to a new house. He tells you that he is nervous about starting at his new school. He invites you to visit his house to help him organise his new bedroom. Write an email to your friend, responding to his news and to his request.

Unit 11

1 **Which of these sentences are correct (C) and incorrect (I)?**

1 If you like challenges, sign up today! C
2 Would you play for them if you can? I
3 When you score, you get one point. C
4 If you get a red card, you stop playing. C
5 If the rain doesn't stop, they cancel the match. I
6 If it'll stop raining, we can go out. I
7 He'd feel better if he got up off that sofa! C
8 If I scored eight goals, I will be a hero! I
9 If I were you, I'd join the team. C
10 The coach won't be happy if we'll lose. I

How many did you get right? ☐

Grammar

Zero conditional

If clause	Main clause
present simple	present simple

We use the zero conditional to talk about the results of an action or situation that are always true. We can use *when* instead of *if*.
If a player gets the ball in the net, she scores a point.
When a player gets the ball in the net, she scores a point.

First conditional

If clause	Main clause
present tense	*will* + infinitive

We use the first conditional to talk about the results of an action or situation that will probably happen now or in the future.
If I **win** the tournament, I**'ll be** very pleased.
If you're going out, we**'ll come** with you.

We can use can, could, may or might in the main clause instead of will. We can also use an imperative.
If Tabitha **does** that again, she **might get** a red card.
If the equipment **isn't** too heavy, **move** it onto the pitch.

Second conditional

If clause	Main clause
past tense	*would* + infinitive

We use the second conditional to talk about the results of an action or a situation:
• that probably won't happen now or in the future.
I **would be** fitter if I **started** running.
• that we know will not happen now or in the future.
If Grandma won the marathon, she**'d be** on social media everywhere!

We can also use the second conditional to give advice.
If I **were** you, I**'d join** the basketball team. It's really fun.

We can use could or might in the main clause instead of would.
Sally **could** win the race if she tried harder.
If you went now, you **might** get tickets for the match.

> **Note**
> We usually use *were* for all persons in second conditional sentences.
> If Dad **were** here, he'd be proud.

11

unless

We can use *unless* in conditional sentences. It means the same as *if not*.
*Luke won't play tennis tomorrow **unless** it's a nice sunny day.*
*I wasn't allowed to go to training practice **unless** I finished my homework.*

Grammar exercises

2 Use the prompts to write zero conditional sentences.

1 water / freeze – you / put it in the freezer
   Water freezes if / when you put it in the freezer.

2 you / score points – you / put the ball through the basket
   You score points if / when you put the ball through the basket.

3 you / boil water – it / become steam
   If / When you boil water, it becomes steam.

4 you / mix white and red – you / get pink
   If / When you mix white and red, you get pink.

5 milk / become sour – you / leave it out of the fridge
   Milk becomes sour if / when you leave it out of the fridge.

6 you / be out in the sun for too long – you / become unwell
   If / When you are out in the sun for too long, you become unwell.

7 you / put ice in water – it / float
   If / When you put ice in water, it floats.

8 babies / cry – they / get hungry
   Babies cry if / when they get hungry.

3 Read the sentences. Then use the prompts to write first conditional sentences.

1 I don't want to wear my helmet. (you / get hurt)
   If you don't wear your helmet, you'll get hurt.

2 Let's play a little longer. (we / miss the bus home)
   If we play a little longer, we'll miss the bus home.

3 I don't want to go to practice. (you / not improve your skills)
   If you don't go to practice, you won't improve your skills.

4 We want to go to the stadium. (we / see some famous footballers)
   If we go to the stadium, we'll see some famous footballers.

5 They want to start playing tennis. (they / be fitter)
   If they start playing tennis, they'll be fitter.

6 He doesn't drink any water during training. (he / feel tired)
   If he doesn't drink any water during training, he'll feel tired.

7 Let's get tickets for the basketball match. (we / not have money for the concert)
   If we get tickets for the basketball match, we won't have money for the concert.

8 She doesn't want to train for the race. (she / not win)
   If she doesn't train for the race, she won't win.

4 Match the problem (1–8) with the advice (a–h). Then write sentences with *you* and the first conditional.

1 be thirsty — [d]   **a** catch the bus on time
2 feel cold — [c]   **b** eat something healthy
3 not want to damage your feet — [e]   **c** put on a jumper
4 be hungry — [b]   **d** drink some water
5 hurt your leg — [g]   **e** wear a good pair of trainers
6 be tired — [h]   **f** work really hard
7 want to win — [f]   **g** see a doctor
8 not want to be late for the race — [a]   **h** take a short break

1 *If you're thirsty, drink some water.*
2 *If you feel cold, put on a jumper.*
3 *If you don't want to damage your feet, wear a good pair of trainers.*
4 *If you're hungry, eat something healthy.*
5 *If you hurt your leg, see a doctor.*
6 *If you're tired, take a short break.*
7 *If you want to win, work really hard.*
8 *If you don't want to be late for the race, catch the bus on time.*

5 Rewrite the sentences with *if* or *unless*.

1 The coach may ask you to leave the team unless you stop shouting at everyone.
The coach may ask you to leave the team if you don't stop shouting at everyone.

2 If Stella doesn't work harder, the coach won't let her play on Saturday.
Unless Stella works harder, the coach won't let her play on Saturday.

3 Unless you get enough exercise, you might develop health problems.
If you don't get enough exercise, you might develop health problems.

4 They'll miss the start of the tournament unless they leave right now.
They'll miss the start of the tournament if they don't leave right now.

5 If he doesn't score soon, we'll take him off the pitch.
Unless he scores soon, we'll take him off the pitch.

6 My coach will be disappointed unless I go to every training session.
My coach will be disappointed if I don't go to every training session.

7 If you don't wear your helmet, you can't go cycling.
Unless you wear your helmet, you can't go cycling.

8 If I don't start eating well, I could get ill.
Unless I start eating well, I could get ill.

6 Rewrite the sentences with the second conditional.

1 I don't have a bike, so my dad has to drive me to the events.
If I had a bike, my dad wouldn't have to drive me to the events.

2 He doesn't get much exercise, so he isn't very fit.
If he got more exercise, he would be fitter.

3 She isn't good at scoring goals, so the coach doesn't pick her for the team.
If she were / was good at scoring goals, the coach would pick her for the team.

4 We don't have money, so we can't buy new football shirts.
If we had money, we could buy (some) new football shirts.

5 We don't have enough players, so we'll need to cancel the match.
If we had enough players, we wouldn't need to cancel the match.

6 The fans don't have tickets, so they can't enter the stadium.
If the fans had tickets, they could enter the stadium.

7 The coach is busy, so I have to train on my own today.
If the coach weren't / wasn't busy, I wouldn't have to train on my own today.

8 It's raining, so they can't do their practice session this evening.
If it weren't / wasn't raining, they could do their practice session this evening.

Sentence transformation

7 Complete the second sentence so that it has a similar meaning to the first sentence, using the word given. Do not change the word given. You must use between two and five words.

1 Mixing green and red paint together gives you purple.
You get purple _____ *when you mix* _____ green and red paint together. **WHEN**

2 My advice is that you don't join the basketball team.
If I _____ *were you I wouldn't / would not* _____ join the basketball team. **WERE**

3 She needs to hurry up – she's going to miss the bus.
She'll miss the bus _____ *unless she hurries* _____ up. **UNLESS**

4 Dean doesn't practise much, which could be why he doesn't win many matches.
If Dean _____ *practised more, he might not* _____ lose as many matches. **MIGHT**

5 You could be fitter, but you are lazy.
If you _____ *were not lazy* _____ , you could be fitter. **NOT**

6 Running for too long gives me a headache.
I get a headache _____ *if I run* _____ for too long. **IF**

7 He often breaks his racket because he hits the ball very hard.
If he didn't hit the ball very hard _____ *he wouldn't / would not break* _____ his racket as often. **WOULD**

8 If you don't sleep well at night, stop drinking coffee.
If you stop drinking coffee _____ *you'll / you will sleep better* _____ at night. **BETTER**

Vocabulary

Phrasal verbs

8 Choose the correct option (a–b).

1 *meet up with* means
  - (a) see someone after planning to do so
  - b do things that someone wants you to do

2 *fall over* means
  - a break into pieces
  - (b) fall to the ground

3 *try out* means
  - a put on a piece of clothing
  - (b) test to see what something is like

4 *show someone around* means
  - (a) lead someone through a place
  - b lead someone into a room

5 *warm up* means
  - a put on heavy clothes
  - (b) prepare your body for exercise

6 *cheer someone on* means
  - a make someone happy
  - (b) encourage someone loudly

7 *go down as* means
  - (a) be remembered as
  - b have a bad fall

8 *kick off* means
  - (a) start
  - b move

9 Complete the sentences with the correct form of the phrasal verbs from Exercise 8.

1 Our team may _____ *go down as* _____ one of the worst volleyball teams in history!
2 The snowboarder was about to cross the finish line when she _____ *fell over* _____ and hurt her leg.
3 I think the judo competition _____ *kicks off* _____ at four o'clock, so don't be late.
4 Steve usually _____ *warms up* _____ for about ten minutes before he goes for a run.
5 I'm interested in joining your gym. Can someone _____ *show me around* _____ , so I can see the equipment?
6 He decided to _____ *try out* _____ a yoga class to help him deal with his anxiety.
7 Athletes appreciate it when fans come to watch them and _____ *cheer them on* _____ .
8 Let's _____ *meet up with* _____ Lola at the weekend. We can go for a coffee after swimming.

11

Exam practice

Multiple-choice cloze

10 For each question, choose the correct answer.

1 She ___ the ball into the back of the net.

   A ran   **B** caught   **C** scored   **(D)** shot

2 If he makes it round the race ___ more than once, I'll be surprised!

   A pool   **B** pitch   **(C)** track   **D** court

3 You can't play hockey unless you've got a ___ .

   (A) stick   **B** racket   **C** bat   **D** bow

4 It's important to wear ___ when you're snowboarding – it gets cold out there!

   A life jackets   **B** skates   **(C)** gloves   **D** boards

5 She's amazing in the water. She can ___ like a fish.

   (A) swim   **B** play   **C** sail   **D** ride

6 You're a really good artist; if you enter the drawing ___ , you might win.

   A championship   **(B)** competition   **C** race   **D** tournament

7 I'm not interested in ___ sports like basketball; I prefer sports where we play one-on-one.

   A indoor   **B** individual   **(C)** team   **D** athletic

8 The weather outside is terrible. Let's ___ a workout at home.

   A run   **B** make   **C** play   **(D)** do

Open cloze

11 For each question, write the correct answer. Write one word for each gap.

1 If you played a team sport, you ___*would*___ learn some useful skills.

2 Let's go skating at the ice ___*rink*___ at the weekend. It'll be fun.

3 I wouldn't even think about entering the marathon if I ___*were*___ you. You aren't fit enough.

4 In archery you need a bow and ___*arrow*___ , which you use to hit a target.

5 When you ___*score*___ a goal, you get one point.

6 She trains twice a week and plays ___*for*___ a local football team on Saturdays.

7 They like all kinds of ___*ball*___ sports, from tennis and golf to cricket and rugby.

8 The gymnastics coach is amazing – all the gymnasts at the club are ___*in*___ very safe hands.

Speaking

12 Work in pairs. Discuss the questions.

- What happens if you don't eat properly?
- What will happen if you don't do exercise?
- What would you do if you were unfit?
- If you were a famous athlete, who would you be? Why?

Unit 12

Awareness

1 Which of these sentences are correct (C) and incorrect (I)?

1 We could have bought tickets if we wouldn't have spent all our money.   _I_

2 If they had invited you to play, would you have joined them?   _C_

3 Teddy wishes he might play for the first team.   _I_

4 If only there was a place to go climbing in the area.   _C_

5 She wishes she would be as fit as her sister.   _I_

6 Would you wish you had trained harder for the competition?   _I_

7 If I arrived at the track earlier, the coach might have let me race.   _I_

8 If he had had a mountain bike, he would have entered the event.   _C_

9 I wish the fans wouldn't shout at me every time I make a mistake.   _C_

10 Dad wishes he hadn't left the cricket team when he was at university.   _C_

How many did you get right? ☐

Grammar

Third conditional

If clause	Main clause
past perfect tense	*would* + have + past participle

We use the third conditional to talk about events or situations in the past that could have happened, but didn't. These are always hypothetical things because we cannot change the past.
*If they **had won** the competition, they **would have received** the gold medal.* (They didn't win the competition, so they didn't receive the gold medal.)

We can use *could* or *might* in the main clause instead of *would*.
*We **could have played** for the team if we had trained harder.*
*If the tracksuit had been better quality, Juan **might have bought** it.*

wish and *if only*

We use *wish* to talk about a situation or an action we aren't happy about, or to say how we would like something to be different.
We use *wish* + a past tense when we talk about the present or the future.
*She **wishes** she **were** better at paddleboarding.*

We use *wish* + a past perfect tense when we talk about the past.
*We **wish** we **had looked after** our health better when we were young.*

We use *wish* + *would* + infinitive when we talk about other people's annoying habits or to say that we would like something to be different in the future. We use it for actions, not states. We can only use *wish* + *would* when the subjects are different.
*I **wish** my brother **would stop** taking my helmet without asking me first.*
*Tina **wishes** she **could take part** in the athletics event.*

We can use *If only* instead of *wish* in affirmative and negative sentences.
***If only** there **was** a swimming pool in our school.*
***If only** I **wasn't** so slow. I can't join the running team.*

12

Grammar exercises

2 **Match the beginnings of the sentences (1–8) with their endings (a–h).**

1	He wouldn't have missed the chance to go diving	*d*	**a**	I could have gone paddleboarding.
2	If she hadn't hurt her leg this morning,	*b*	**b**	she would have gone to the gym.
3	If she hadn't been such a lazy teammate,	*e*	**c**	if they had won the final match.
4	If the game hadn't been so boring,	*h*	**d**	if he hadn't woken up feeling ill.
5	They might have won the whole tournament	*c*	**e**	the others would have liked her more.
6	I might have taken the coaching job	*g*	**f**	would you have bought them?
7	If it hadn't been my parents' wedding anniversary,	*a*	**g**	if the salary had been better.
8	If the gloves hadn't been so expensive,	*f*	**h**	we would have stayed to see the end.

3 **Complete the sentences with the third conditional form of the verbs. Sometimes more than one answer is possible.**

1 If he _____*hadn't been*_____ (not / be) in such a hurry, he _____*wouldn't have left*_____ (not / leave) his hockey stick at home.

2 She _____*would have bought*_____ (buy) tickets for the game if she _____*had remembered*_____ (remember) earlier.

3 If they _____*hadn't been*_____ (not / be) so tired, they _____*would have come*_____ (come) sailing.

4 Helen _____*wouldn't / might not have felt*_____ (not / feel) weak if she _____*had eaten*_____ (eat) something earlier.

5 They _____*would have been*_____ (be) warmer if they _____*had taken*_____ (take) their tracksuits.

6 If I _____*had worked*_____ (work) harder, I _____*wouldn't have disappointed*_____ (not / disappoint) my coach.

7 If he _____*had felt*_____ (feel) stronger, _____*would / could he have won*_____ (he / win) the marathon?

8 If our team _____*had raised*_____ (raise) more money, we _____*would / could have got*_____ (get) nicer shirts.

4 **Use the prompts to write sentences with the third conditional.**

1 Toby / not / play so badly, / coach / not / take him off the team
   If Toby hadn't played so badly, the coach wouldn't have taken him off the team.

2 I / not / fall on the ice, / not / hurt my head
   If I hadn't fallen on the ice, I wouldn't have hurt my head.

3 Sonia and David / have enough money, / go to the last Olympics
   If Sonia and David had had enough money, they would have gone to the last Olympics.

4 Karen / not / eat so unhealthily, / get ill?
   If Karen hadn't eaten so unhealthily, would she have got ill?

5 Peter / not / win a medal, / his coach / be disappointed?
   If Peter hadn't won a medal, would his coach have been disappointed?

6 I / take my swimming costume / go swimming
   If I had taken my swimming costume, I would have gone swimming.

7 We / not / like sports / not / join the school handball team
   If we didn't like sports, we wouldn't have joined the school handball team.

8 Mum and Dad / see me play / be very proud of me
   If Mum and Dad had seen me play, they would have been very proud of me.

5 Read the paragraph, then write sentences with the third conditional.

> Anna wanted to watch a game of baseball, so she went to the local field. She saw that a player on the team wasn't playing. She asked to play. Anna scored a lot of runs. A manager noticed her. He asked her to join his team. The team won the championship. Anna became a star athlete.

1 *If Anna hadn't wanted to watch a game of baseball, she wouldn't have gone to the local field.*
2 *If she hadn't gone to the local field, she wouldn't have seen that a player on the team wasn't playing.*
3 *If the player on the team had been playing, she wouldn't have asked to play.*
4 *If she hadn't asked to play, she wouldn't have scored a lot of runs.*
5 *If she hadn't scored a lot of runs, a manager wouldn't have noticed her.*
6 *If the manager hadn't noticed her, he wouldn't have asked her to join his team.*
7 *If the manager hadn't asked her to join his team, the team wouldn't have won the championship.*
8 *If the team hadn't won the championship, Anna wouldn't have become a star athlete.*

6 Coach Young is getting annoyed with his team. Use the prompts and *I wish* to write what the coach says.

1 Elias / not play so dangerously
   I wish Elias wouldn't play so dangerously.

2 Julia / be on time for the training sessions
   I wish Julia would be on time for the training sessions.

3 Layla and Sara / not forget their uniforms all the time
   I wish Layla and Sara wouldn't forget their uniforms all the time.

4 Brett / not shout at his teammates
   I wish Brett wouldn't shout at his teammates.

5 Victor / have better coordination
   I wish Victor had better coordination.

6 Sam / listen my instructions
   I wish Sam would listen to my instructions.

7 Jon and Gina / can understand the rules
   I wish Jon and Gina could understand the rules.

8 Sonia / be stronger and faster
   I wish Sonia were / was stronger and faster.

7 Complete the conversations with the correct form of the verbs.

1 **A:** Do you know it's only two o'clock?
   B: I know! I wish we ____*could leave*____ (leave), but we've got a meeting until five o'clock.
2 **A:** Tom hurt his leg. He wishes he ____*had warmed up*____ (warm up) before he went for a run.
   B: Yes, if only he ____*had asked*____ (ask) us about that. Warming up is really important.
3 **A:** Why does Jane look so miserable?
   B: Oh, she wishes she ____*could play*____ (play) on her brother's football team.
4 **A:** What's the matter, boys?
   B: We can't take part in the race. If only we ____*weren't*____ (not be) so unfit.
5 **A:** I wish we ____*could go*____ (go) paddleboarding more often.
   B: Yes, if only there ____*was*____ (be) a river closer to home.
6 **A:** It's still raining.
   B: Yes, I wish it ____*would stop*____ (stop). I want to go to the outdoor swimming pool.

12

Vocabulary

8 Complete the table.

Noun	Verb	Adjective	Adverb
1 _athletics_ / athlete	–	athletic	athletically
2 _challenge_	challenge	challenged / challenging	challengingly
competition / competitor	3 _compete_	competitive	competitively
coordination / coordinator	coordinate	4 _coordinated_ / coordinating	coordinately
danger	5 _endanger_	dangerous / endangered / endangering	dangerously
depth	deepen	6 _deep_	deeply
diving / 7 _diver_	dive	diving	–
freedom	free	free	8 _freely_
improvement	9 _improve_	improved / improving	–
strength	strengthen	10 _strong_	strongly

9 Complete the sentences with words from Exercise 8.

1 He wishes he had better hand-eye _coordination_ . Every time he tries to catch the ball, he drops it!
2 My best friend is very _athletic_ – she's really good at lots of sports.
3 You need to calm down – breathe _deeply_ for a minute.
4 My sister is very _competitive_ and gets very upset if she loses.
5 I think free _diving_ is one of the most dangerous sports in the world – I wouldn't want to try it.
6 The cyclists are in _danger_ of crashing if they don't slow down.
7 The coach worked on a new and _improved_ training plan to help his team win the tournament.
8 Doing workouts at the gym can help you _strengthen_ your body.
9 The marathon was really _challenging_ for me, but I'm glad I did it.
10 Don't you love the feeling of freedom _freedom_ you get when you're skiing down a mountain?

Exam practice

10 For each question, write the correct answer. Write one word for each gap.

1 At school we only play cricket in the summer, but we play football all _year_ round.
2 When I went waterskiing, I fell in the water every time the boat pulled me _along_ .
3 He _does_ gymnastics on Tuesdays and Thursdays.
4 Have you ever heard _of_ a sport called korfball?
5 Joe is taking part _in_ both the 100 and 200-metre races.
6 When you go snowboarding, you can reach speeds of _up_ to fifty kilometres per hour.
7 They're always doing watersports. I don't think they like being _on_ land!
8 She's very good _at_ archery. She hits the target almost every time.

Multiple-choice cloze

11 **For each question, choose the correct answer.**

1 If you'd like to try out free diving, you need to find a professional diving ___ .
A athlete   **B** diver   **(C)** instructor   **D** competitor

2 Many athletes train in hotter countries so that they learn to cope ___ the heat.
A at   **(B)** with   **C** for   **D** on

3 She went to the shopping mall to buy a new swimming ___ .
(A) costume   **B** suit   **C** uniform   **D** dress

4 Are you going to carry ___ taking private tennis lessons?
A about   **(B)** on   **C** around   **D** in

5 The player tried to score, but the ball hit the goal ___ .
A area   **B** stick   **(C)** post   **D** net

6 The rider was very experienced and knew how to deal ___ difficult horses.
(A) with   **B** of   **C** by   **D** after

7 I can't ___ my breath for more than a minute.
(A) hold   **B** keep   **C** lose   **D** take

8 We go to the gym just ___ fitness – we don't enjoy it at all!
A about   **B** to   **C** in   **(D)** for

Writing

12 **Read the writing task and write your answer in about 100 words. Try to use language for giving opinions, reasons and examples.**

Some people believe that students should spend much more time at school doing sport and fitness. Others think that students should spend most of their time doing academic subjects. What do you think about the amount sport and fitness at school? Give examples to support your answer.

Grammar

1 Choose the correct option to complete the conversations.

1 **A:** Oh no! It's starting to snow.
  B: You're right! *Are you going to /* (*Will you*) tell Joe to come indoors, please?

2 **A:** Look at that skier. He's out of control!
  B: He *will /* (*'s going*) to hit that tree!

3 **A:** Do you know your plans for the future?
  B: Yes. I *will /* (*'m going*) to become a professional tennis player.

4 **A:** How old is your sister?
  B: She *'s going to /* (*will*) be twelve next Friday.

5 **A:** Why did you and your friends make a mess in the house?
  B: I'm sorry, Dad. I promise I *'m not going to /* (*won't*) do it again.

6 **A:** Have they fixed your heating yet?
  B: No. But I'm sure they (*'ll*) */ 're going to* finish very soon.

7 **A:** What's your parents' schedule like for next week?
  B: They *'ll /* (*'re going*) to travel to Asia.

8 **A:** I've decided to try a new sport.
  B: Really? Which one (*are you going to*) */ will you* try?

2 Complete the sentences with the present simple or the present continuous form of the verbs.

1 **A:** You look excited, Sally.
  B: I am. I _____'m playing_____ (play) in the hockey tournament this afternoon!

2 What _____'s Ana doing_____ (Ana / do) tomorrow evening?

3 The yoga class _____starts_____ (start) at two o'clock.

4 When _____'s the new table arriving_____ (the new table / arrive)?

5 **A:** Will your coach be at the match next week?
  B: No. She _____'s going_____ (go) to the USA for a sports conference.

6 **A:** Can Tim play tennis later?
  B: No, he _____'s working_____ (work) all evening.

7 Their train _____leaves_____ (leave) at seven o'clock.

8 Harry's football training _____finishes_____ (finish) at 8.00 tonight. Don't forget.

9 **A:** Why are Karl and Jen so busy these days?
  B: Because they _____'re moving_____ (move) into their new bungalow at the weekend.

10 **A:** Do you know the opening hours of the swimming pool?
   B: Yes, it _____opens_____ (open) at 8 a.m. and _____closes_____ (close) at 10 p.m.

3 **Choose the correct option (a–b) to complete the sentences.**

1 I'll never finish the housework this morning ___ you help me.

   (a) unless   **b** if

2 Marco ___ so unhealthy if he got more exercise.

   (a) wouldn't be   **b** won't be

3 You know, Priya, if I ___ you, I wouldn't buy that flat; it's too expensive.

   a am   **(b)** were

4 Water ___ when temperatures drop below zero degrees.

   a will freeze   **(b)** freezes

5 If you aren't busy later, ___ to my house and I'll cook you dinner.

   a would come   **(b)** come

6 If you change that jacket, you ___ that you look much smarter.

   (a) will see   **b** would see

7 If you hurry, you ___ to the stadium in time for the match.

   a get   **(b)** will get

8 If they ___ harder, they might do better in competitions.

   (a) tried   **b** would try

9 What ___ if he won a lot of money?

   a will Tom do   **(b)** would Tom do

10 If we finish work early, ___ to the cinema.

   (a) we will go   **b** we would go

4 **Complete the sentences with one word for each gap.**

1 I wish I __*could*__ afford to move into a bigger house.

2 Stan wishes he __*had*__ asked his parents for advice before he made his decision.

3 If __*only*__ Nancy had won the tennis match; she would have been so pleased.

4 If I had known you were sleeping, I would __*not*__ have called you.

5 I wish there __*were*__ more skilled players on my team!

6 They hope the weather __*will*__ get colder; they want to go skiing!

7 Would you __*have*__ joined the team if the coach had asked you?

8 I wish the neighbours __*would*__ stop playing football in our back garden.

9 He's __*going*__ to join the local tennis club next month.

10 Katherine is getting a puppy, but I wouldn't __*if*__ I were her!

5 **Choose the correct option to complete the sentences.**

1 What time *does* / *will* maths start on Tuesdays? I can't remember.

2 I wish my brother *stopped* / *would stop* talking about how strong he is!

3 The fans will be thrilled if we *will score* / *score* one more goal.

4 Unless you stop shouting at the players, the coach *is going to ask* / *will ask* you to leave the team.

5 They *'re going* / *go* onto the pitch soon.

6 Susie wishes she *had* / *had had* a better bike; hers is very old.

7 When I'm older, I'm *going to learn* / *learning* how to snowboard.

8 The ice on the river is very thin. Those skaters *will* / *are going* to fall through it!

9 If Jim *hadn't missed* / *wouldn't miss* the penalty, we would have won the match.

10 If only we *had bought* / *bought* tickets last week; now there aren't any left.

6 **Tick the correct sentences. Then correct the mistakes. Sometimes more than one answer is possible.**

1 The builders will start work on the tennis court next week.

   The builders are starting / are going to start work on the tennis court next week.

2 If I'm doing the housework this afternoon, I won't be able to cook dinner.

   ✓

3 Don't worry, Coach Myers. I'm sure we are going to play in the finals.

   Don't worry, Coach Myers. I'm sure we'll play in the finals.

4 I don't know where Tim is. If only he tells me where he was going before he left the house!

   I don't know where Tim is. If only he had told me where he was going before he left the house!

5 If he had known you were trying to a buy flat, he would give you some useful advice.

   If he had known you were trying to buy a flat, he would have given you some useful advice.

6 We will move house next month; we've bought a flat.

   We're moving / going to move house next month; we've bought a flat.

7 My parents have decided they are going to move away from the city.

   ✓

8 If the baby is hungry, she's crying.

   If the baby is hungry, she cries.

9 Look at those black clouds. It'll rain.

   Look at those black clouds. It's going to rain.

10 If we go for a run every day, we would be much fitter – but of course that will never happen!

   If we went for a run every day, we would be much fitter – but course that will never happen!

Use of English

Word formation

7 Use the word in capitals to form a word that fits in the gap.

1 She's good at most sports because she's got great _____coordination_____ .   **COORDINATE**
2 What workout can I do to help _____strengthen_____ my legs?   **STRONG**
3 The coach hopes his team can _____compete_____ in next year's league.   **COMPETITION**
4 I'm going to decorate my living room at the weekend. It's a huge room, so it'll be bit quite _____challenging_____ .   **CHALLENGE**
5 Moving to the countryside was the best thing we did – we can walk ___ _freely_ ___ without all the traffic.   **FREEDOM**
6 They're really interested in health and _____fitness_____ .   **FIT**
7 If we get to the _____championship_____ , I'll be so happy!   **CHAMPION**
8 Jon isn't interested in _____athletics_____ ; he prefers watersports.   **ATHLETE**

Sentence transformation

8 Complete the second sentence so that it has a similar meaning to the first sentence, using the word given. Do not change the word given. You must use between two and five words.

1 I've arranged to see my university friends for lunch.
   I'm _____meeting up with_____ my university friends for lunch.   **UP**

2 My niece, who is an excellent swimmer, is the one in the orange swimming costume.
   My niece, who can _____swim like a fish_____ , is the one in the orange swimming costume.   **FISH**

3 The excited fans shouted loudly, giving encouragement to their favourite player.
   The excited fans _____cheered on_____ their favourite player.   **ON**

4 Can you stop breathing for two minutes?
   Can you _____hold your breath_____ for two minutes?   **HOLD**

5 The new manager will look after the team – he's excellent.
   The team _____is in safe hands_____ – the new manger is excellent.   **SAFE**

6 I'd like to come out, but I'm cleaning the house all afternoon.
   I'd like to come out, but I'm _____doing the housework_____ all afternoon.   **DOING**

7 You and your brother can bake a cake if you keep the kitchen clean and tidy.
   If you don't _____make a mess_____ in the kitchen, you and your brother can bake a cake.   **MESS**

8 The match starts at three o'clock, so don't be late.
   The match _____kicks off_____ at three o'clock, so don't be late.   **OFF**

Grammar

9 For questions 1–10, choose the word or phrase that best completes the sentence.

1 ___ her flat for the rest of the afternoon?
- **(A)** Is she cleaning
- **B** Will she clean
- **C** Does she clean
- **D** Would she clean

2 If only my neighbours ___ loud music all day.
- **A** won't play
- **B** haven't played
- **(C)** didn't play
- **D** did play

3 Traffic is very bad, so we ___ !
- **A** are going be late
- **B** will be late
- **(C)** are going to be late
- **D** are late

4 Metal turns orange if you ___ it in the rain.
- **(A)** leave
- **B** will leave
- **C** are leaving
- **D** are going to leave

5 They ___ the kitchen if they hadn't been busy.
- **A** can paint
- **B** could paint
- **C** would paint
- **(D)** could have painted

6 We ___ to the finals if we win this match.
- **A** would get
- **(B)** will get
- **C** would have got
- **D** won't get

7 I ___ be late for practice again, I promise.
- **A** am not going to
- **B** will
- **(C)** won't
- **D** am going to

8 It would be better if they ___ a bigger flat.
- **(A)** had
- **B** have
- **C** will have
- **D** are having

9 Next week, we ___ in the golf tournament.
- **A** play
- **(B)** are playing
- **C** going to play
- **D** will play

10 Unless you train, you ___ play.
- **A** are able to
- **B** will be able to
- **C** might be able to
- **(D)** won't be able to

Vocabulary

10 For questions 11–20, choose the word or phrase that best completes the sentence.

11 Before we start, let's warm ___ .
- **A** on
- **(B)** up
- **C** down
- **D** out

12 I prefer ___ sports to individual sports.
- **(A)** team
- **B** ball
- **C** outdoor
- **D** fitness

13 If only I didn't need to ___ all the housework.
- **A** have
- **B** make
- **C** deal
- **(D)** do

14 To play baseball, you need a baseball ___ .
- **A** stick
- **B** racket
- **(C)** bat
- **D** board

15 It's nice when fans are there to ___ you on.
- **A** carry
- **B** shout
- **(C)** cheer
- **D** try

16 Can you put the dishes ___ in the cupboard?
- **(A)** away
- **B** out
- **C** down
- **D** about

17 Come in! I can ___ you around.
- **(A)** show
- **B** visit
- **C** move
- **D** have

18 In winter, we use a thicker ___ at night.
- **A** pillow
- **B** sheet
- **(C)** duvet
- **D** cushion

19 The show kicks ___ at 4 p.m.
- **A** in
- **(B)** off
- **C** on
- **D** out

20 I'm hot. I'm going to ___ a shower.
- **A** get
- **B** do
- **C** make
- **(D)** have

Unit 13

Awareness

1 **Which of these sentences are correct (C) and incorrect (I)?**

1 We can borrow your camera, can't we? _C_
2 This isn't an interesting place? _I_
3 She hasn't got much luggage, hasn't she? _I_
4 They're visiting the coast, aren't them? _I_
5 'Who did went to Argentina?' 'Susan went to Argentina.' _I_

6 The boat leaves at four o'clock, doesn't it? _C_
7 Those are expensive flights, aren't they? _C_
8 Let's go out for dinner, shall we? _C_
9 Didn't Karen come with you? She said she would! _C_
10 You check the dates before you booked the accommodation, didn't you? _I_

How many did you get right? ☐

Grammar

Question tags

Question tags are short questions at the end of a positive or negative sentence. They are formed with a modal or an auxiliary verb + a personal pronoun.

We usually use an affirmative question tag after a negative sentence, and a negative question tag after an affirmative sentence.
*We **aren't** happy with this hostel, **are** we?*
*He's in South America at the moment, **isn't** he?*

When the main sentence has an auxiliary verb, we use the same auxiliary verb in the tag.
*You **haven't** tried rock climbing before, **have** you?*
*The travellers **are** looking for a cheap place to stay, **aren't** they?*

When the main sentence has a modal verb, we use the same modal verb in the tag.
*They **can't** travel without a visa, **can** they?*

When the main sentence contains a verb in the present simple or the past simple, we use *do / does, don't / doesn't* and *did / didn't* in the question tag.
*You **like** travelling by train, **don't** you?*
*He **went** on a wildlife safari, **didn't** he?*

We use question tags when we want:
• someone to agree with what we are saying.
*It's a dangerous city, **isn't it?***
• to make sure that what we are saying is right.
*The scuba-diving lesson starts at one o'clock, **doesn't it?***

Subject and object questions

When who, what, or which asks about the subject of a question, the word order stays the same as in an affirmative sentence.
***Who went** horse riding at the holiday camp?*
*(**Jen and Oliver** went horse riding.)*

When who, what, or which are the object of a question, the word order changes in the question form.
***What did** Jen and Oliver **do** at the holiday camp?*
*(They went **horse riding**.)*

> **Note**
>
> Some question tags are irregular. Notice the way these tags are formed.
> *I **am** a sociable person, **aren't I?***
> *Everyone **is** coming on the trip, **aren't they?***
> ***Let's** take the mountain path, **shall we?***
> ***Don't** forget to text me when you get there, **will you?***
> ***Be** quick, **won't you?***
> ***This / That** is so exciting, **isn't it?***
> ***These / Those** are interesting traditions, **aren't they?***

13

Negative questions

We use negative questions:

- to express surprise.

Didn't Stella **go** on holiday to Scotland with her family? (No, she's started a new job.)

- in exclamations.

Isn't this the best beach on the planet?

- when we expect the listener to agree with us.

Wasn't that a boring journey?

To answer negative questions, we just use a Yes or No answer depending on what we think. A Yes answer agrees with a negative question; a No answer disagrees with a negative question.

Isn't cycling a fun sport?

Yes. / Yes, it is. (= agreement) **No. / No, it isn't.** (= disagreement)

Grammar exercises

2 **Choose the correct option to complete the sentences.**

1 You aren't going to the airport now, _are you_ / aren't you?

2 You've been snowboarding before, have you / _haven't you_?

3 He'll call me when he gets to Peru, will he / _won't he_?

4 Your uncle hasn't received his new passport yet, _has he_ / hasn't he?

5 On holiday, they eat out every day, do they / _don't they_?

6 I'm much more relaxed now, am I / _aren't I_?

7 She didn't give you your boarding pass, _did she_ / didn't she?

8 Look at my new suitcase. It's great, is it / _isn't it_?

3 **Match the sentences (1–10) with their question tags (a–j).**

1	He's never been to Indonesia,	_i_	**a** can't he?
2	She's an experienced pilot,	_e_	**b** didn't she?
3	Let's go paddleboarding,	_h_	**c** didn't they?
4	Peter can free dive,	_a_	**d** will you?
5	I'm fit enough to go hiking,	_f_	**e** isn't she?
6	Don't do anything silly,	_d_	**f** aren't I?
7	Hally booked her adventure holiday,	_b_	**g** are they?
8	Everyone had a great time,	_c_	**h** shall we?
9	Those people aren't here for the boat trip,	_g_	**i** has he?
10	You've paid the bus fare,	_j_	**j** haven't you?

4 **Write question tags for the sentences.**

1 Let's do something exciting, _shall we_?

2 This is the end of the tour, _isn't it_?

3 Don't leave your sunglasses on the boat, _will you_?

4 Nancy is anxious about flying, _isn't she_?

5 Everyone is coming to the museum, _aren't they_?

6 Paul doesn't play golf anymore, _does he_?

7 This coach isn't very comfortable, _is it_?

8 They had fun surfing, _didn't they_?

9 I'm going to have an amazing experience, _aren't I_?

10 Those aren't expensive headphones, _are they_?

5 Choose the correct option (a–b).

1 Which travel company did Sam recommend to Tina?
   a Tina recommended a local travel company to Sam.
   b Sam recommended a local travel company to Tina.

2 Who took Pedro to the hotel?
   a Pedro took Gemma to the hotel.
   b Gemma took Pedro to the hotel.

3 Who asked Luke to come on the walking tour?
   a Luke asked Tim to come on the walking tour.
   b Tim asked Luke to come on the walking tour.

4 What was in the luggage?
   a The small backpack was in the luggage.
   b The luggage was in small backpack.

5 Who was the noisy passenger shouting at?
   a The noisy passenger was shouting at the flight attendant.
   b The flight attendant was shouting at a noisy passenger.

6 What did Lyra buy you?
   a Lyra bought me a souvenir from Italy.
   b I bought Lyra a souvenir from Italy.

7 Who likes wildlife?
   a Wildlife likes me.
   b I like wildlife.

8 What is Sara doing for her friend?
   a Her friend is organising a surprise party for Sara.
   b Sara is organising a surprise party for her friend.

6 Write subject questions for the answers.

1 *Who likes to go on cruise ships?*
   Joe likes to go on cruise ships.

2 *Who was talking about the castle?*
   The tour guide was talking about the castle.

3 *Who went camping with Dad?*
   Francis went camping with Dad.

4 *Who borrowed the racket?*
   Jan borrowed the racket.

5 *Who asked the passengers to put on their seatbelts?*
   The pilot asked the passengers to put on their seatbelts.

6 *Who is taking a taxi to the airport?*
   Michael is taking a taxi to the airport.

7 *Who tried out archery for the first time?*
   Ted tried out archery for the first time.

8 *Who decided to buy a new camera?*
   My cousin decided to buy a new camera.

13

7 Complete the second sentence so that it has a similar meaning to the first sentence, using the word given. Do not change the word given. You must use between two and five words.

1 The plane didn't arrive on time, did it?

The plane _____ *arrived late* _____ , didn't it?   **LATE**

2 I'm a difficult passenger, aren't I?

I'm ____ *not an easy passenger, am* ____ I?   **EASY**

3 Could you pass me your luggage, please?

Please ____ *pass me your luggage, will* ____ you?   **WILL**

4 It isn't always easy to communicate when you're abroad, is it?

Sometimes, it _____ *can be difficult* _____ to communicate when you're abroad, can't it?   **DIFFICULT**

5 You've got the train tickets, haven't you?

You ____ *didn't / did not forget* ____ the train tickets, did you?   **FORGET**

6 She won't miss the ferry to France, will she?

She _____ *will catch* _____ the ferry to France, won't she?   **CATCH**

7 We wish there was more time for us to travel south.

If we ____ *had more time, we would* ____ travel south, wouldn't we?   **HAD**

8 What about going for a hike?

Let's _____ *go hiking, shall* _____ we?   **HIKING**

Vocabulary

8 Complete the collocations and expressions with these nouns.

| add | change | go | have | make | prepare | suffer | take |

1 __*prepare*__ for a journey   **5** __*take*__ time off

2 __*change*__ your mind   **6** __*go*__ on a day trip

3 __*suffer*__ from over-tourism   **7** __*make*__ a hotel reservation

4 __*have*__ a good time   **8** __*add*__ to your carbon footprint

9 Complete the sentences with the correct form of the expressions from Exercise 8.

1 Bali in Indonesia has ____ *suffered from over-tourism* ____ for several years.

2 They're _____ *having a good time* _____ on their camping holiday, aren't they? They won't want to come back!

3 He flew to five different countries last year, which hugely ____ *added to his carbon footprint* ____ .

4 He was planning to travel by sea to get to Argentina, but he _____ *changed his mind* _____ when he saw how long it would take.

5 You'd like to _____ *go on a day trip* _____ to the coast, wouldn't you?

6 If only I could _____ *take time off* _____ ; but work is just too busy at the moment.

7 You have ____ *made a hotel reservation* ____ , haven't you? I don't want to arrive in Berlin with nowhere to stay!

8 She thinks it takes about a month to _____ *plan for a journey* _____ around the world.

Exam practice

Open cloze

10 For each question, write the correct answer. Write one word for each gap.

1 There's no more space left in our suitcase, ____*is*____ there?

2 Please make sure you wake up ____*on*____ time! The plane leaves at nine o'clock.

3 It took five hours to get to the holiday home – there was a huge ____*traffic*____ jam on the road.

4 Isn't he afraid of flying ____*in*____ a helicopter?

5 I would love to travel around the whole country ____*by*____ rail.

6 People live and work in an Oxford college. Tourists aren't ____*free*____ to go everywhere.

7 She didn't want her holiday to end, ____*did*____ she?

8 They waited ____*at*____ the bus stop for ages before the bus arrived.

Multiple-choice cloze

11 For each question, choose the correct answer.

1 On the way to the ferry, we stopped for fuel at the ___ station.
  A train   B bus   **C** petrol   D fire

2 They're really looking forward ___ their holiday in Vietnam.
  A on   B for   C with   **D** to

3 She decided to book a tour as she didn't want to travel ___ the country on her own.
  A around   B along   C onto   D by

4 While he was living in Brazil, he moved in ___ a family so he could learn Portuguese.
  A for   **B** with   C around   D to

5 I would love to go to Australia to see my grandparents, but I can't ___ it at the moment.
  A afford   B pay   C buy   D cost

6 Please ___ out of your room by midday and leave the key at reception.
  A look   **B** check   C leave   D exit

7 At times, the climber found it difficult to ___ motivated.
  A rest   **B** stay   C wait   D save

8 Try not to take too much ___ when you go on holiday; try to travel light.
  A backpack   **B** baggage   C suitcase   D handbag

13

Speaking

12 **Work in pairs. Look at the two photos and discuss the questions.**

- What people can you see in the photo?
- Where are they?
- What do they look like?
- What are they doing?
- What's the weather like?
- What time of day is it?
- What can you see in the background?
- Which place in the photos would you prefer to go to? Why?

1 Which of these sentences are correct (C) and incorrect (I)?

1 Sara wasn't been scuba diving for very long.   ___I___

2 I had been walking for hours and had fallen over just before reaching the town.   ___I___

3 We hadn't been in the cave for long before they found us.   ___C___

4 Had they been waiting since very long?   ___I___

5 The boat trip had already begun when the storm started.   ___C___

6 We had realised afterwards that we had been very lucky.   ___I___

7 When the diver saw a shark, he quickly took some photos.   ___C___

8 They paid for the tickets and entered the castle.   ___C___

9 She had been swimming in the sea for a while before her friend had been joining her.   ___I___

10 How long had you looking for the museum?   ___I___

How many did you get right? ☐

Grammar

Past perfect simple

Affirmative	Negative	Questions
I / He / She / It / We / You / They **had ('d)** visit**ed**.	I / He / She / It / We / You / They **had** not (**hadn't**) visit**ed**.	**Had** I / he / she / it / we / you / they visit**ed**?
Short Answers		
Yes, I / he / she / it **had**. **Yes**, we / you / they **had**.	**No**, I / he / she / it **hadn't**. **No**, we / you / they **hadn't**.	

Spelling: talk → talk**ed**, dance → danc**ed**, travel → travel**led**, tidy → ti**died**, stay → stay**ed**

> **Note**
>
> Some verbs are irregular and do not follow these spelling rules. See a list of irregular verbs on pages 158–159.

We use the past perfect simple for an action or situation that finished before another action, situation or time in the past.
*The hiker **had been** alone in the rainforest for hours before his group found him.*

> **Note**
>
> We often use these common time expressions with the past perfect simple: *already, for, for a long time / ages, just, never, once, since 2017 / June, so far, yet*, etc.
> *The snow had **already** begun to fall when we got to the lake.*

Past simple and past perfect simple

In some sentences, it is clear which action happens first. In this case, we can use the past simple for both actions. However, when the order of events is not clear, or when we want to emphasise which action happened first, we can use the past perfect simple for the first action.
*They **went** to the café and **talked** about the holiday.*
*She **realised** that she **had been** unkind to her friend.*

Remember that we must use the past simple for both actions when one past action happens quickly after another or one is the immediate result of the other.
*When the tour guide **started** talking, everyone **listened**.*

Past perfect continuous

Affirmative	Negative	Questions
I / He / She / It / We / You / They **had ('d) been** visit**ing**.	I / He / She / It / We / You / They **had not (hadn't) been** visit**ing**.	**Had** I /he / she / it / we / you / they **been** visit**ing**?
Short Answers		
Yes, I / he / she / it **had.** **Yes**, we / you / they **had.**	**No**, I / he / she / it **hadn't.** **No**, we / you / they **hadn't.**	

Spelling: take → tak**ing**, swim → swi**mming**, study → stud**ying**

We use the past perfect continuous for:

- actions that started in the past and were still in progress when another action started or when something happened.

*He **had been waiting** for ages to see some wildlife before he could take a photo of some lions.*

- actions that were in progress in the past and had an effect on a later action.

*They **had been swimming** for over an hour in the sea and started to feel cold.*

> **Note**
>
> We often use these common time expressions with the past perfect continuous: *all day / night / week, for years / a long time / ages, since.* We can use *How long ...?* with the past perfect continuous in questions and *for (very) long* in questions and negative sentences.
> *Stan had been going surfing **for years**.*
> ***How long** had you been taking part in marathons by then?*

Grammar exercises

2 **Complete the sentences with the past perfect simple form of the verbs.**

1 We _____*had returned*_____ (return) home before the rain started.
2 Parina _____*had never ridden*_____ (never / ride) a horse before, but she realised she was good at it.
3 _____*Had they already gone*_____ (they / already / go) to the station by the time you arrived?
4 Until 2019, we _____*had never been*_____ (never / go) sailing.
5 The children _____*hadn't tried*_____ (not / try) out the park's biggest zipline yet.
6 I _____*had worked*_____ (work) as an instructor for ages and was bored with my job.
7 Dean and Freya _____*had hiked*_____ (hike) in the mountains and told many stories about it.
8 _____*Had Karl bought*_____ (Karl / buy) the surf board when he lost his credit card?

3 Sam went on a diving holiday last month. What had he done before he went on holiday? Use the prompts and the past perfect simple to write questions and answers.

1 buy / some scuba-diving equipment
   Q: _____*What had Sam bought*_____ before he went on holiday?
   A: _*He had bought some scuba-diving equipment.*_

2 book / his flight
   Q: _____*What had Sam booked*_____ before he went on holiday?
   A: _*He had booked his flight.*_

3 research online / about diving centres
   Q: _*What had Sam researched online*_ before we went on holiday?
   A: _*He had researched online about diving centres.*_

4 learn / water safety skills
   Q: _*What had Sam learned / learnt*_ before he went on holiday?
   A: _*He had learned / learnt water safety skills.*_

5 ask to take / time off work
   Q: _*What had Sam asked to take*_ before he went on holiday?
   A: _*He had asked to take time off work.*_

6 pack / his bags
   Q: _____*What had Sam packed*_____ before he went on holiday?
   A: _*He had packed his bags.*_

4 Underline the action which happened first.

1 After <u>Billy had packed his rucksack</u>, he left the house.
2 Gina counted to ten and dived off the cliff into the water.
3 The divers realised later that <u>they had been in great danger</u>.
4 As soon as <u>he got to the hotel</u>, he had a shower.
5 When <u>we had eaten our meal</u>, we paid the bill.
6 By the time we got to the campsite, <u>Mum had put up the tent</u>.
7 <u>I had just moved to Argentina</u> when I got the chance see the Iguazú Falls.
8 The tourists left the castle because <u>the tour had finished</u>.

5 Complete the sentences with the past perfect continuous form of the verbs.

1 My grandfather _____*had been living*_____ (live) in his old house for ages before he moved in with us.
2 I _____*had been travelling*_____ (travel) around the country for months before I decided to live there permanently.
3 _____*Had she already booked*_____ (she / already / book) her holiday when she remembered you wanted to visit?
4 They _____*hadn't been flying*_____ (not / fly) for long when the pilot made an announcement.
5 How long _____*had you been planning*_____ (you / plan) your trip before you booked the ferry?
6 We _____*had been playing*_____ (play) beach volleyball in the rain since noon, so we were very wet.
7 Gillian was calm and relaxed because she _____*had been doing*_____ (do) a yoga course all week.
8 He _____*hadn't been working*_____ (not / work) on the cruise ship for long when he realised he missed dry land.

6 Choose the correct option to complete the sentences.

1 Theo and Jamal had left / had been leaving the airport before I got there.

2 You fell asleep before dinner. Had you had / Had you been having a busy day?

3 I had sailed / had been sailing all morning, so I was exhausted.

4 The boys had been packing / had packed their bags and then they called a taxi.

5 By the time we reached the top of the mountain, the sun had been setting / had set.

6 Frank had a headache because he had been listening / had listened to loud music all afternoon.

7 We hadn't talked / hadn't been talking for long before the café closed.

8 How long had they been looking / had they looked for souvenirs to take home?

7 Tick the correct sentences. Then correct the mistakes.

1 Yesterday was a bad day for me because I hadn't been sleeping well the night before.
Yesterday was a bad day for me because I hadn't slept well the night before.

2 After Dad made breakfast, we had sat down to eat.
After Dad had made breakfast, we sat down to eat.

3 When she flew in a helicopter for the first time, she was sick.
_✓_

4 George hadn't been skiing for long when he fell over and broke his leg.
_✓_

5 Had they been waiting long before the coach had arrived?
Had they been waiting long before the coach arrived?

6 The athlete had been training for hours, so he had felt tired.
The athlete had been training for hours, so he felt tired.

Vocabulary

Prepositions

8 Choose the correct option to complete the phrases.

1 have permission to / for do something

2 be a long way for / from somewhere

3 have a negative effect on / about something

4 tell someone of / about something

5 go on / in a boat trip

6 spend money on / in something / someone

7 travel by / on air

8 stay at / in home

9 book accommodation for / to something

10 go by / on foot

9 Complete the sentences with the correct form of the prepositional phrases from Exercise 8.

1 I've haven't got any plans this weekend – I just want to _____ stay at home _____ and watch TV.

2 She _____ told you about _____ her housewarming party, didn't she?

3 He wouldn't have _____ spent money on _____ a first-class plane ticket, would he?

4 They want to do the 'Camino de Santiago' walk, but it's a long way to _____ go on foot _____ .

5 This visa means that I _____ have permission to _____ enter India.

6 He never used to _____ travel by air _____ because he was afraid of flying.

7 We've _____ booked accommodation for _____ Casablanca and Marrakesh, but not for Rabat yet.

8 Tourism has _____ had a negative effect on _____ the town's beaches – there's plastic rubbish everywhere.

9 I'd been travelling around Asia for months when I realised that I _____ was a long way from _____ home.

10 Her parents had been planning to _____ go on a boat trip _____ , but they went on a bus tour instead.

Exam practice

Open cloze

10 For each question, write the correct answer. Write one word for each gap.

1 _____How_____ long had it been raining before it finally stopped?

2 _____By_____ the time they reached the top of the mountain, they were very tired.

3 The cruise ship had around 3000 passengers _____on_____ board.

4 They visited Antarctica only _____once_____ , in 2018, and they've never wanted to go back.

5 We'd only been travelling since the beginning of the month _____when_____ Beth got ill.

6 I had been looking for my passport _____all_____ morning before I found it in an old suitcase.

7 _____Just_____ as the girls were beginning to get worried, the taxi arrived.

8 He had been a pilot _____for_____ years and was very experienced.

Multiple-choice cloze

11 For each question, choose the correct answer.

1 Travelling around Europe is easier now because many countries share the same ___ .
A money
(B) currency
C cash
D credit

2 Would it be OK to ___ your phone for a minute? I've left mine at home.
(A) borrow
B rent
C hire
D take

3 It took a while to ___ the border from the USA to Mexico.
A walk
B travel
(C) cross
D move

4 She didn't have enough money for the train ___ , so she had to take the bus.
A price
B payment
C cost
(D) fare

5 As they went through ___ , officers stopped them and searched their baggage.
A duty free
(B) customs
C gate
D boarding

6 After travelling around the world, Australia was my nephew's final ___ .
(A) destination
B location
C place
D station

7 You can never balance ___ the negative effects of flying.
A in
B to
C by
(D) out

8 We don't like camping, but some places have wooden ___ , which are great!
A homes
(B) cabins
C hotels
D campsites

Writing

12 Read the writing task and write your answer in about 100 words. Try to use narrative tenses (past simple, past continuous, past perfect simple and past perfect continuous).

Your English teacher has asked you to write a story. Your story must begin with this sentence:
The friends had decided to book the holiday of a lifetime.

1 Which of these sentences are correct (C) and incorrect (I)?

1 My grandfather can making beautiful things out of wood. ⟂

2 It can't be Paul – that man isn't tall enough. C

3 I must do a sailing course in the summer, but I'm not sure yet. ⟂

4 You ought wear a helmet when you go cycling to protect your head. ⟂

5 They must be in Paris. Look – they're standing outside the Louvre Museum. C

6 Do you think I should get Jake a new camera for his birthday? C

7 They might to go to the cinema tonight, if Cara gets home on time. ⟂

8 We shouldn't leaving Ben's house too late as we've got college tomorrow. ⟂

9 I'll be able to drive you to the gym tonight, but not tomorrow night. C

10 I may or may not be able to come to the housewarming party; I need to check my diary first. C

How many did you get right? ☐

Grammar

Modals and semi-modals (1)

can, could and *be able to* for ability

We use *can* + infinitive to talk about general ability in the present and the future.
She **can make** beautiful dresses.

We use *could* + infinitive to talk about general ability in the past (past form of can).
I **could swim** before I **could walk**.

We use *be able to* to talk about:
* ability
I **will be able to** come to the theatre tonight.
She **won't be able to** go skiing – she's hurt her leg.
* a single, specific ability in the past. (It is not possible to use *could* here.)
Were they **able to** go to the concert last night?

should, shouldn't, and *ought to* for advice and suggestions

We use *should* or *shouldn't* (*should not*) + infinitive:
* to give advice or a suggestion.
People of all ages **should exercise** *regularly.*
You **shouldn't drink** *coffee in the evening.*
We **should go** *for a walk later.*
* to ask for advice.
What **should I do** *about reducing stress in my life?*

Note

Ought to can also be used to give advice, but it is not usually used in the question form.
You **ought to** *finish your homework before you go out.*
Shouldn't *you finish your homework before you go out?*

---

could, may, might, must and *can't* for possibility and certainty

We use *could* + infinitive to talk about possibility.
*We **could go** paddleboarding tomorrow, if the weather's good.*

We use *may* + infinitive and *might* + infinitive to talk about a possibility in the future.
*I **may start** a new hobby in the new year.*

We use *must* + infinitive to show that we are sure something is true.
*My brother **must be** excited about winning a gold medal.*

We use *can't* + infinitive to show that we are sure that something isn't possible or true.
*That **can't be** Lauren! She's on holiday this week, isn't she?*

> **Note**
> We can also use *could* for suggestions.
> *We **could** go to the ballet. What do you think?*

Grammar exercises

2 How are the modal and semi-modal verbs used in these sentences? Choose from the list below. You need to use some of them more than once.

> advice   general ability in the present   general ability in the past   something possible in the future
> something not possible   something almost certain   specific ability in the past   suggestion

1 That can't be my art teacher; he's in Florence at the moment.
  something not possible

2 We could try out the school drama club – I think it would be fun.
  suggestion

3 She's been training hard all day. She must be exhausted.
  something almost certain

4 He can play squash very well.
  general ability in the present

5 I could walk when I was only nine months old.
  general ability in the past

6 You ought to see a doctor about your headaches, Dad.
  advice

7 Mum may join the gym next month, but she's still thinking about it.
  something possible in the future

8 He couldn't speak any Spanish until he moved to Seville.
  general ability in the past

9 We were able to see the match – we got tickets at the last minute.
  specific ability in the past

10 They might visit their friends in Germany next year.
   something possible in the future

3 Tick the correct sentences. Then correct the mistakes.

1 They forgot to take their water bottles to football practice, so they should be thirsty.
   They forgot to take their water bottles to football practice, so they must be thirsty.

2 He could visit his grandad in hospital last night.
   He was able to visit his grandad in hospital last night.

3 We couldn't go shopping later – what do you think?
   We could go shopping later – what do you think?

4 You shouldn't work all the time. You need to take a break.
   ✓

5 We must do a sculpture course next term, or perhaps we'll do a painting course.
   We might / may do a sculpture course next term, or perhaps we'll do a painting course.

6 I couldn't ride a bike until I was eight.
   ✓

7 What can't I do when I finish college? I need some advice.
   What should I do when I finish college? I need some advice.

8 We can or can't go away this weekend, so we haven't booked anything yet.
   We may / might or may / might not go away this weekend, so we haven't booked anything yet.

9 That can be true about Julia and Max; they would never split up.
   That can't be true about Julia and Max; they would never split up.

10 He can't speak Japanese very well – but it doesn't stop him trying!
   ✓

4 Choose the correct option to complete the sentences.

1 If you want to get fit, you *must* / (*ought*) to go to the gym.
2 My headphones (*must*) / *can* be broken; I can't hear anything.
3 Fran (*may*) / *should* take sculpture lessons, but it isn't definite.
4 That (*must*) / *may* be Harriet in the café – she always wears those yellow boots.
5 I *may not* / (*can't*) pay for tennis lessons this month as I don't have enough money.
6 You *couldn't* / (*shouldn't*) spend so long playing computer games without taking a break.
7 I'm sorry, that just (*can't*) / *isn't able to* be true – I don't believe you.
8 She's feeling much better, so she'll (*be able to*) / *could* sing in tonight's concert.

5 Complete the sentences with these modal and semi-modal verbs.

be able to	can	can't	could	may	must	ought to	shouldn't

1 You _shouldn't_ work all the time. Why not try out a new hobby?
2 Vic and Ed won't _be able to_ go to the theatre tonight – they don't have a babysitter.
3 We _ought to_ go for a run later, as we've done nothing all day!
4 We _could_ go to the cinema later. There's a film I'd like to see.
5 What he said about Julia learning to water-ski _can't_ be right. She hates water!
6 Do you think children _can_ use social media safely?
7 He _must_ be out. All the lights are off.
8 I _may_ start swimming again, but I'm not sure if I have time.

6 Chose the correct option to complete the sentences.

1 We ___ go cycling today; it's too icy and it'll be dangerous.
   a couldn't   (b) shouldn't   c might not

2 He ___ play any musical instruments, but he's a great singer.
   a might   b must   (c) can't

3 If you don't like ball sports, ___ you try watersports instead?
   a must   b may   (c) couldn't

4 She's just fallen over and she isn't getting up. She ___ be hurt.
   (a) must   b can   c should

5 They ___ to open the window if they're feeling hot.
   a could   (b) ought   c can

6 You and your brother ___ go to the gallery this afternoon if you haven't got any plans.
   a must   b might   (c) could

7 After a tough start, Stefan ___ beat the other player.
   a should   (b) was able to   c could

8 That ___ be our instructor; he's teaching in Brazil.
   (a) can't   b shouldn't   c couldn't

Sentence transformation

7 Complete the second sentence so that it has a similar meaning to the first sentence, using the word given. Do not change the word given. You must use between two and five words.

1 My advice is that you do not miss this play.
   You _____ *should see* _____ this play.   **SEE**

2 If I were you, I'd make better use of my spare time.
   You _____ *ought to* _____ make better use of your spare time.   **TO**

3 We got there in time because we found a taxi.
   We _____ *were able to get* _____ there in time because we found a taxi.   **ABLE**

4 I am really sure that this is a Picasso sculpture.
   This _____ *must be* _____ a Picasso sculpture.   **BE**

5 His cooking was bad when he was younger, wasn't it?
   He _____ *couldn't / could not cook* _____ very well when he was younger, could he?   **COOK**

6 Dean can't finish work early today.
   Dean _____ *will not be able to* _____ finish work early today.   **WILL**

7 How about going backpacking next year?
   We _____ *could go* _____ backpacking next year.   **COULD**

8 They could win the league if they trained harder.
   If they trained harder, winning the league _____ *might be* _____ possible.   **MIGHT**

15

Vocabulary

Word formation

8 **Choose the correct option to complete the sentences.**

1 We watched in (awe) / awesome / awesomeness as he played the piano recital.
2 Going for long walks in the countryside gives my parents a lot of please / (pleasure) / pleasant.
3 You might (enjoy) / enjoyment / enjoyable the new play at the theatre.
4 We were watching a film when the doorbell rang; it gave us such a frighten / frightening / (fright).
5 The idea of singing in public would terror / (terrify) / terrible my brother.
6 You must see that ballet. The dancers will amazing / (amaze) / amazed you!
7 That's a great (photograph) / photography / photographic. You're very talented!
8 She likes to (scare) / scared / scary her little sister by inventing stories about strange animals.

9 **Use the word in capitals to form a word that fits in the gap.**

1 He wants to go caving for his birthday, but we think it's a _____ terrible _____ idea! **TERROR**
2 The music at the classical concert was _____ pleasant _____ , but it wasn't my favourite. **PLEASE**
3 They love watching _____ scary _____ films. **SCARE**
4 He's interested in studying _____ photography _____ at college. **PHOTOGRAPH**
5 This new video game is the most _____ awesome _____ one ever! **AWE**
6 She went mountain biking for the day, but she didn't find it _____ enjoyable _____ . **ENJOYMENT**
7 My dad really likes cooking and he makes some _____ amazing _____ food. **AMAZE**
8 Getting trapped in a lift must be quite a _____ frightening _____ experience. **FRIGHTEN**

Exam practice

Multiple-choice cloze

10 **For each question, choose the correct answer.**

1 They ___ ballet every Saturday morning.
  A a play   **B** some   **C** go   (**D**) do

2 I always listen to ___ when I do the housework – I learn all kinds of things.
  A music   (**B**) podcasts   **C** news   **D** instruments

3 Please don't stay ___ late tonight – you've got school tomorrow.
  (**A**) up   **B** in   **C** off   **D** on

4 It's easy to spend hours watching video ___ on the internet.
  A pieces   **B** cuts   (**C**) clips   **D** bits

5 The theatre director wants to put ___ a play about the life of Shakespeare.
  A in   **B** out   **C** off   (**D**) on

6 Dad can't ___ playing computer games; he'd much prefer to read a book.
  (**A**) stand   **B** give   **C** set   **D** join

7 She wants to study graphic ___ at university.
  A drawing   **B** painting   (**C**) design   **D** diagram

8 The artwork at the exhibition was a bit ___ , but I liked it.
  A awful   (**B**) unusual   **C** difficult   **D** dangerous

11 For each question, write the correct answer. Write one word for each gap.

1 He gets _____a_____ bit annoyed when we interrupt him.

2 I would like to try windsurfing. It _____must_____ be so much fun.

3 They borrowed some money to buy concert tickets, but they promised to pay us _____back_____ the next day.

4 You ought _____to_____ buy a good bike if you want to join the cycling club.

5 Asking our sister to cook us dinner is probably her _____worst_____ nightmare.

6 Why are you still playing computer games if you're tired? You _____should_____ go to bed!

7 The _____thing_____ she likes most about doing sports is playing with others.

8 We don't really like drawing and painting; we prefer _____taking_____ photos.

Speaking

12 Work in pairs. Discuss these things with your partner.

- two things you were able to do last week
- two things you could do when you were five years old
- two things you know you should do but you don't
- two things you can do now that you really enjoy
- two activities or hobbies that you may do when you get older

Awareness

1 **Which of these sentences are correct (C) and incorrect (I)?**

1 I can't come to the art exhibition at the weekend – I may work a shift at the supermarket. ⊥

2 Can Benjamin and I go swimming tomorrow, Mum? C

3 We mustn't go near the oven – it's hot. C

4 You should wear a seatbelt when driving because it's the law. ⊥

5 You really must visit the Alhambra Palace in Spain. It's amazing! C

6 Must I borrow your pen? ⊥

7 Could you mind closing that window? It's really cold in here. ⊥

8 You need to bring lots of food to the party – I've got enough snacks for everyone and a huge cake. ⊥

9 She said she might come to visit us next weekend. C

10 You don't have to come to the drama club, but I think you'll enjoy it. C

How many did you get right? ☐

Grammar

Modals and semi-modals (2)

can, *could*, *may*, *might* and *would* for permission and requests

We use *can* + infinitive for:
• permission.
*Visitors **can go** into this part of the museum if they pay for a ticket.*
• requests.
***Can** you **help** me fix my bike?*

We use could + infinitive for polite requests.
***Could** you **take** a photo of us, please?*

We use may + infinitive for:
• polite permission.
*You **may leave** the classroom when you have finished the test.*
• polite requests.
***May** I **borrow** your paddleboard?*

We use *might* + infinitive:
• for very polite permission.
***Might** I **have** another slice of cake?*
• as the past tense of requests with may.
*He asked if he **might borrow** her tennis racket.*

We use *would* + infinitive for very polite requests.
***Would** you **open** the window, please?*

Remember that *would* is also used for actions that we did regularly in the past, but that we don't do now (see Unit 4, page 20).
*He **would always read** a story to the children before they went to sleep.*

must, mustn't and have to for necessity, obligation and prohibition

We use *must* + infinitive to:
• say something is necessary.
*You **must be** at the sports club by five o'clock.*
• talk about obligations.
*You **must have** a driving licence if you want to drive.*
• to strongly recommend something.
*You really **must go** to the exhibition. It's amazing!*

We use *mustn't* (*must not*) + infinitive to talk about something that is not allowed.
*People **mustn't park** their cars in front of the door.*

We use *have to* to:
- say that something is necessary.

*You **have to** practise playing the piano for an hour a day.*
- talk about obligation.

*We **have to** take a survival course before we do the sailing course.*

needn't and *don't have to* for lack of obligation or necessity

We use *needn't* (*need not*) + infinitive to say that something is not necessary. We don't use it in affirmative sentences.
*You **needn't take** food to the get-together because our parents are doing a barbecue.*

We use *don't have to* + infinitive to show that there is no obligation or necessity.
*You **don't have to play** football with us this weekend if you're too busy.*

Note

We can also use *need* as an ordinary verb. It has affirmative, negative and question forms and it is usually used in the present simple and the past simple. It is followed by *to* + infinitive.
*Ed **needs to get** a better camera.*
*The children **didn't need to walk** to the swimming pool because Dad took them in the car.*
*Did he **need to buy** tickets before the match?*

Grammar exercises

2 Match the sentences (1–10) with their meanings (a–j).

1	Can I borrow your pencil for a minute?	h	a	a very polite request
2	You must be at squash practice every week.	c	b	something that happened in the past
3	Teenagers can join the photography club.	i	c	it's necessary
4	They asked if they might have some water.	f	d	a strong recommendation
5	You don't have to go on that course.	g	e	it isn't allowed
6	Would you book a table for dinner, please?	a	f	a very polite request in the past
7	You really must buy those trousers!	d	g	it isn't necessary
8	You mustn't talk loudly in the library.	e	h	a request
9	He would always jog early each morning.	b	i	it's allowed
10	Do we have to wear safety equipment?	j	j	Is it an obligation?

3 Choose the correct option to the complete the sentences.

1 *Needn't* / Can we take our drinks into the theatre?
2 Could / *Must* you speak a bit louder, please?
3 She wants to know if she *needn't* / may join the poetry club.
4 You must / *can* have a licence to fly a plane.
5 Did they *have* / need to pay for the extra tennis lesson?
6 We don't have to / *can't* go to bed early – tomorrow is Saturday!
7 I must / *would* finish my homework by Wednesday; Thursday will be too late.
8 We *need to* / needn't travel late at night. I'll book a daytime flight instead.
9 Must / Might we have some more water, please?
10 You really *need* / must read this book. You'll love it.

4 **Match the beginnings of the sentences (1–8) with their endings (a–h).**

1 Tom has to train at `d`
2 We mustn't forget `e`
3 You don't have `a`
4 May I `c`
5 She asked if they might `f`
6 Can Lola come `b`
7 Would you `h`
8 They needn't `g`

a to study tonight if you're too tired.
b camping with us in the school holidays?
c speak to the manager, please?
d the swimming pool every morning.
e to book the hotel room.
f come for dinner on Saturday.
g take their own skates – they can hire them.
h buy some more paint when you're town?

5 **Complete the sentences with these modal and semi-modal verbs.**

| can | have to | might | must (x2) | mustn't | needn't | would |

1 You really ___must___ try windsurfing. It's awesome!
2 He ___needn't___ wear a suit – casual clothes are fine.
3 Fred, ___can___ you pass me that scarf?
4 I ___must___ revise for the exam, or I'll fail it!
5 Does she ___have to___ travel a lot for work?
6 Excuse me, sir, ___would___ you please pass me one of those bags?
7 We asked if we ___might___ borrow some money to go shopping.
8 The children ___mustn't___ go outside when it's dark.

6 **Rewrite the sentences with modals and semi-modal verbs. Sometimes more than one answer possible.**

1 There is no obligation for you to come to the club meeting tomorrow.
   You don't have to / You needn't come to the club meeting tomorrow.

2 Her mum used to write a poem for her birthday every year.
   Her mum would write a poem for her birthday every year.

3 Hey Joe, is it OK if I use your bike for a few minutes?
   Hey Joe, can / could I use your bike for a few minutes?

4 It isn't necessary to pay for tickets – it's a free event.
   You don't have to / needn't pay for tickets – it's a free event.

5 People are allowed to go into the gallery now if they want.
   People can / may go into the gallery now if they want.

6 Would you open the door for me, please?
   Could you open the door for me, please?

7 It's necessary for all players to follow the rules of the game.
   All players must / have to follow the rules of the game.

8 The students are not allowed to use their mobile phones in class.
   The students mustn't use their mobile phones in class.

7 Choose the correct option (a–c) to complete the sentences.

1 When I was young, I ___ run for an hour every evening.
a can
(b) would
c might

2 Students ___ use the school theatre without permission from Ms Devon.
(a) mustn't
b needn't
c have to

3 You ___ come early; I'll have lots of help before the party starts.
(a) needn't
b mustn't
c wouldn't

4 She hurt her leg, but luckily she ___ go to hospital.
a couldn't
b may not
(c) didn't have to

5 ___ you help me with this equipment, please?
a Need
(b) Could
c Must

6 You ___ go to the park, but please be home in time for dinner.
(a) can
b might
c must

7 ___ you spend some time with Grandad this weekend? He misses you.
a Must
b Need
(c) Would

8 He asked if he ___ rent our spare room.
(a) might
b may
c must

Vocabulary

Phrasal verbs

8 Match the phrasal verbs (1–8) with their meanings (a–h).

1	come round	*b*	a	become part of a group activity
2	get along with	*d*	b	go to someone's house
3	get together	*h*	c	give something to a person in authority
4	give up	*g*	d	be friendly with
5	hang out	*f*	e	begin a new activity
6	join in	*a*	f	spend time with people
7	hand in	*c*	g	stop doing something
8	take up	*e*	h	meet in order to spend time together

9 Complete the sentences with the correct form of the phrasal verbs from Exercise 8.

1 They have to _____*hand in*_____ their application forms for the course by Monday.

2 Would she be interested in _____*taking up*_____ a more challenging sport like windsurfing?

3 A few friends from drama club are _____*coming round*_____ for lunch. Would you like to join us?

4 They _____*gave up*_____ ballet a month ago. They really didn't enjoy it.

5 I don't understand why Max isn't _____*joining in*_____ . He usually loves playing volleyball.

6 He's been backpacking around Europe for the last three months, so he wants to _____*get together*_____ with his family at the weekend.

7 She remembers the first time she met Ana at university; she _____*got along with*_____ her immediately and they've been best friends ever since.

8 We haven't got much planned this weekend – we'll probably just relax and _____*hang out*_____ with our friends.

16

Exam practice

10 For each question, write the correct answer. Write one word for each gap.

1 The children love ball sports such ____as____ tennis, basketball and cricket.

2 ____Can____ we go to the theatre at the weekend, Mum?

3 I really want to ____go____ on a surfing course in the summer.

4 You ____must____ see the wildlife photography exhibition. It's absolutely fascinating!

5 She ____asked____ if I wanted to join the photography club.

6 Do you need ____to____ take a break? You look tired.

7 Would you buy some materials ____for____ my art project, when you go shopping?

8 He's interested ____in____ poetry and drama.

Multiple-choice cloze

11 For each question, choose the correct answer.

1 I think we should have classes that develop our creativity; ___ instance, learning to play a musical instrument or doing graphic design.

    A to   **B** in   **(C)** for   **D** at

2 Every evening he spends hours ___ the internet.

    A swimming   **(B)** surfing   **C** sailing   **D** running

3 I can't stand it when people don't switch ___ their mobile phones at the cinema.

    (A) off   **B** to   **C** in   **D** out

4 What did you think of the actor's ___ in the play?

    (A) performance   **B** presentation   **C** recital   **D** drama

5 She doesn't just like ballet, she ___ it.

    A dislikes   **B** hates   **C** quite likes   **(D)** adores

6 You mustn't throw rubbish ___ the lake as it will pollute the water.

    A on   **B** at   **(C)** into   **D** around

7 The students asked the headteacher if they might ___ a recycling campaign at school.

    A go   **B** enter   **C** be   **(D)** start

8 I love that film; it's really ___ with very strange and funny characters.

    A A frightening   **(B)** crazy   **C** awful   **D** difficult

Writing

12 Read the writing task and write your answer in about 100 words. Try to use linking words and phrases.

The editor of the school magazine has asked you to write an article recommending two or three hobbies that young people may want to take up in their free time. Give reasons for your recommendations.

Grammar

1 Complete the paragraph with the past simple, past perfect simple or the past perfect continuous form of the verbs. Sometimes more than one answer is possible.

a Two years ago, my grandfather, Joe, ¹ _____retired_____ (retire) from his company after he
² ___he had been working / had worked___ (work) there for over 50 years. For a few weeks after that, he
³ _____searched_____ (search) for something to do in his free time. He ⁴ __hoped / was hoping__ (hope) to
find a hobby that would get him fit, but as he ⁵ ___had never been___ (never / be) very athletic, he
⁶ _____knew_____ (know) it was going to be difficult to find a sport that ⁷ _____was_____ (be)
right for him. Only last week, he called me to say that he ⁸ _____had found_____ (find) a sport he could
take up. Now he plays walking football, and he loves it!

b Last summer, my family and I ⁹ _____went_____ (go) on a trip to Canada. All of us
¹⁰ ___had been looking___ (look) forward to our visit for ages and we all ¹¹ _____had_____ (have) an
amazing time while we were there. As 1st July is Canada Day, my cousin ¹² _____wanted_____ (want) us
to watch the river boat races on the East River, which is near her house. I ¹³ _____had seen_____ (see)
boats before, of course, but it was the first time I ¹⁴ ___had ever seen___ (ever / see) a river boat.
It ¹⁵ _____was_____ (be) a very colourful event! The river boat races ¹⁶ _____were_____ (be)
something I'll never forget.

2 Choose the correct option to complete the sentences.

1 Clean up the mess once you've finished painting, won't you / don't you?
2 **A:** What was in her suitcase?
   B: Her handbag / suitcase was in her suitcase / handbag.
3 I'm going to enjoy rock climbing, aren't I / will I?
4 **A:** Who invited Sonia to Marek's barbecue?
   B: Marek / Sonia invited Marek / Sonia to the barbecue.
5 **A:** You're / Aren't you Max Smith?
   B: Yes, I am.
6 Let's go to the photo exhibition this evening, won't I / shall we?
7 **A:** Which tennis racket did Jay borrow from Arif?
   B: Jay / Arif borrowed the expensive tennis racket.
8 **A:** Didn't Karen go / Karen didn't go to summer camp?
   B: No, she did / didn't.

3 Choose the correct option to complete the sentences.

1 If you get bored today, you may / should call me.
2 We can go swimming later, can / can't we?
3 Those trainers are very expensive, aren't / doesn't they?
4 I'm not certain, but I think George ought / might be at the pool.
5 Gia couldn't / mustn't move the piano; it's too heavy and she'll hurt herself.
6 We don't have to / must not buy uniforms; the team will provide them.
7 Who did ask / asked Van to join the book club?
8 It's / Isn't it an amazing play?
9 I had never been skied / skied until March this year.
10 Grandpa should / would come home and cook dinner every evening.

4 **Choose the correct option (a–b) to complete the sentences.**

1 If you've hurt your foot, you ___ to see a doctor.
  (a) ought
  b should

2 ___ we eat in the living room?
  a Needn't
  (b) Can we

3 Dad ___ come sailing this weekend, but he's still thinking about it.
  (a) may
  b shouldn't

4 My grandmother ___ always do some gardening on summer evenings.
  (a) would
  b needs

5 Did you ___ pay for the concert tickets or were they free?
  (a) need to
  b have

6 I ___ make dinner tonight – we're eating out!
  a couldn't
  (b) don't have to

7 I ___ be back before dark or my parents will get worried.
  a am able to
  (b) must

8 That ___ be my uncle; he's working abroad at the moment.
  a mustn't
  (b) can't

9 I took some time off work, so I ___ to take the children to the cinema.
  (a) was able
  b could

10 You ___ wear your life jacket on the boat.
  (a) must
  b could

5 **Read these situations and complete the sentences using a suitable modal verb. Sometimes more than once answer is possible.**

1 **A:** I don't know where my baseball bat is.
  B: Well, it ___*can't*___ be at the pitch – the coach checked before we left.

2 **A:** I'm so hungry I'm going to eat this whole pizza.
  B: I really don't think you ___*should / ought to*___ ; you'll make yourself ill.

3 **A:** Your mum isn't working tomorrow, is she?
  B: No, she isn't. She ___*could*___ stay in bed if she wanted to, but she always likes to get up early.

4 **A:** Let's go to the sports centre, shall we?
  B: Sorry, but I ___*mustn't / can't*___ do any exercise at the moment – I've hurt my back.

5 **A:** What shall we bring to the party? How about some snacks?
  B: You ___*needn't / don't have to*___ bring anything – just bring yourselves!

6 **A:** Are they coming round to our house at the weekend?
  B: I asked them if they ___*might / could / would*___ come, but they need to check.

7 **A:** I've just finished my workout at the gym. I was there for two hours!
  B: You ___*must*___ be exhausted!

8 **A:** Do you need anything from the shop?
  B: ___*Can / Could / Would*___ you get a bunch of bananas and some milk, please?

9 **A:** Did you see your cousin yesterday?
  B: Yes, I ___*was able to*___ meet her for lunch.

10 **A:** I'm going to work now.
  B: Do you ___*have to*___ work every weekend?

6 **Find one mistake in each sentence. Then correct the mistakes.**

1 The athlete who was winning suddenly fell over and, as a result, I could win the marathon.
The athlete who was winning suddenly fell over and, as a result, I was able to win the marathon.

2 The winner was swimming since she was a young child.
The winner had been swimming since she was a young child.

3 Everyone from the judo club got a new uniform, don't they?
Everyone from the judo club got a new uniform, didn't they?

4 They've been working on their project all day, so they needn't be tired.
They've been working on their project all day, so they must be tired.

5 As soon as they had been hearing the window smash, they called the police.
As soon as they heard the window smash, they called the police.

6 The team had finally been winning a trophy after months of hard training.
The team had finally won a trophy after months of hard training.

7 You couldn't eat all that chocolate. It'll make you ill.
You shouldn't eat all that chocolate. It'll make you ill.

8 That mustn't be Jordan; he's spending the year backpacking around Europe.
That can't be Jordan; he's spending the year backpacking around Europe.

Use of English

Word formation

7 **Use the word in capitals to form a word that fits in the gap.**

1 She may study graphic _design_ at college – she's very creative.   **DESIGNER**
2 Picasso was a great painter, but he was brilliant at _sculpture_ too.   **SCULPT**
3 That might be one of the most _frightening_ flights I've ever had!   **FRIGHT**
4 Sam isn't sure yet, but he thinks he may start _photography_ at school.   **PHOTOGRAPH**
5 I'm sure the children will love these new books – the stories are _awesome_ !   **AWE**
6 You mustn't let your brother watch anything _scary_ on TV. He'll get nightmares.   **SCARE**
7 They're performing some _poetry_ at the theatre this evening. Shall we go?   **POET**
8 That really wasn't a very _enjoyable_ game. The teams were terrible!   **ENJOY**

Open cloze

8 **For each question, write the correct answer. Write one word for each gap.**

1 You won't change your mind now, _will_ you?
2 He doesn't like the outdoors much and really can't _stand_ camping, especially in the rain!
3 He adores surfing and spent a lot of money _on_ a new board.
4 If you find you have a lot of _free_ time, you could join a sports club.
5 Frank likes all sports and he's just taken _up_ squash.
6 By the _time_ the explorers got back home, they were dirty, hungry and tired.
7 What's the official _currency_ in Australia? Is it the dollar?
8 Could you tell me what time we have to check _out_ of the hotel?

Grammar

9 For questions 1–10, choose the word or phrase that best completes the sentence.

1 We agreed to invite Susie, ___ we?
A did
B will
C didn't
D haven't

2 I'm wrong again, ___ ?
A am I
B aren't I
C isn't it
D shall I

3 Don't forget to call, ___ ?
A will you
B are you
C won't you
D can't you

4 Tom ___ be working; he isn't answering his phone.
A must
B should
C would
D can

5 If you're going to late be for training, you ___ let the coach know in advance.
A should
B ought
C could
D would

6 ___ Marta choose to take up?
A Which did hobby
B Which hobby did
C Which does hobby
D Which hobby does

7 ___ an unusual name?
A She has got
B She hasn't got
C Hasn't she got
D She's not got

8 He ___ an awful day and felt miserable.
A had been having
B had
C had been
D had had

9 That ___ be Joe's place. He doesn't live in a flat.
A mustn't
B wouldn't
C shouldn't
D can't

10 We asked Gloria if she ___ come to the concert.
A must
B might
C ought
D need

Vocabulary

10 For questions 11–20, choose the word or phrase that best completes the sentence.

11 Would you like to come ___ for dinner later?
A in
B round
C about
D to

12 We missed the bus, so we went home ___ foot.
A for
B with
C by
D on

13 They need to ___ a hotel reservation.
A pay
B do
C make
D take

14 It's difficult, but don't ___ up the course.
A hand
B get
C take
D give

15 When did you ___ the border to Mexico?
A along
B across
C cross
D over

16 We can't ___ to go on holiday this year.
A afford
B cost
C price
D borrow

17 Has the area suffered ___ too much tourism?
A for
B from
C by
D in

18 Officers at ___ searched the man's bags.
A duty free
B boarding pass
C customs
D departures

19 He moved ___ with his friends last week.
A round
B on
C over
D in

20 She was ill, so she stayed ___ home.
A in
B at
C about
D on

1 Which of these sentences are correct (C) and incorrect (I)?

1 Many cars are built in Japan. __C__
2 Last night we were followed a complete stranger. __I__
3 An urgent email was sent her. __I__
4 My camera is repaired by my dad last night. __I__
5 These biscuits were baked at the local café. __C__

6 A lot of money was given to the charity. __C__
7 Is the recycling bins collected today? __I__
8 The children were shown how the 3D printer worked. __C__
9 Many people hurt in the road accident. __I__
10 Our computers weren't make in the USA. __I__

How many did you get right? ☐

Grammar

The passive

We use the passive when:

- the action is more important than the person or thing that did the action (the agent).
*The windows **were smashed** during the night.*

- we don't know the agent, or it is not important.
*You can use the laptop again. It **was fixed** this morning.*

We form the passive with the verb *be* + past participle.
*These toys **are produced** in China. The clothes **were taken** to the second-hand shop.*

We change an active sentence into a passive sentence in the following way.

	Object	Subject	
People **produce**	these toys here.	These toys	**are produced** here.
People **produced**	these toys here.	These toys	**were produced** here.

In the examples, we do not know who produced the toys and it is not important.

Note

After some verbs there are two objects, for example, *give, lend, send* and *show*. When we want to change an active sentence with two objects into the passive voice, one becomes the subject of the passive sentence and the other one remains an object. Which object we choose depends on what we want to emphasise.
The structure is:
subject [indirect object] + passive verb + direct object (+ *by* + agent).
*I was given **the headphones** (by my brother).*
OR
subject [direct object] + passive verb + indirect object (+ *by* + agent).
When a direct object is followed by an indirect object, we have to use a preposition (*to, for*, etc.) in front of the indirect object.
*The headphones were given **to me** (by my brother).*

by and with

Sometimes it is important to mention the agent (who or what is responsible for the action) in a passive sentence. We use the word *by* before the agent to do this.
*The dishwasher was invented **by** Josephine Cochran. The house was destroyed **by** a fire.*

Sometimes we want to mention a tool or material in the passive sentence. We use the word *with* to do this.
*The birthday cake was decorated **with** sweets.*

17

Grammar exercises

2 Use the prompts to write sentences with the passive form of the present simple.

1 cars / built / factories
   Cars are built in factories.

2 device / power / batteries
   The device is powered by batteries.

3 tea / grow / Kenya?
   Is tea grown in Kenya?

4 these instructions / not / write / very clearly
   These instructions aren't written very clearly.

5 a lot of cheese / produce / France
   A lot of cheese is produced in France.

6 computers / make / the UK?
   Are computers made in the UK?

7 his songs / not / record / in a studio
   His songs weren't recorded in a studio.

8 office / clean / every evening
   The office is cleaned every evening.

9 engineering / not / teach / schools
   Engineering isn't taught in schools.

10 Tom / never / wake up / his alarm
   Tom is never woken up by his alarm.

3 Complete the sentences with past passive form of the verbs.

1 The money ___*was transferred*___ (transfer) to my bank account the following day.
2 ___*Was the food delivered*___ (the food / deliver) to the house on time last night?
3 Over several years, photos of the planet Mars ___*were taken*___ (take) by rovers.
4 Her smartphone ___*was stolen*___ (steal) last week.
5 He's got an excellent doctor and the problem ___*was dealt*___ (deal) with very quickly.
6 ___*Were the students shown*___ (the students / show) how to build a computer during their visit to the factory?
7 All the urgent emails ___*were responded*___ (respond) to before lunch time.
8 The new security camera ___*was installed*___ (install) yesterday.

4 Rewrite the sentences in the passive.

1 Satellites collect data and send it to Earth.
Data is collected by satellites and sent to Earth / Data is collected and sent to Earth by satellites.

2 A group of engineers developed the robot.
The robot was developed by a group of engineers.

3 A teenager designed the new video game.
The new video game was designed by a teenager.

4 Did his sister teach him how to use that app?
Was he taught how to use that app by his sister?

5 A reliable company transported the hardware.
The hardware was transported by a reliable company.

6 Someone didn't switch off the computer at the end of the day.
The computer wasn't switched off at the end of the day.

7 The team didn't test the software properly.
The software wasn't tested properly by the team.

8 A young company created the new fitness tracker.
The new fitness tracker was created by a young company.

9 Our manager tells us not to send personal emails.
We are told by our manager not to send personal emails.

10 Someone left a strange message on her phone.
A strange message was left on her phone.

11 Do billions of people use the internet?
Is the internet used by billions of people?

12 Someone marked the exam papers incorrectly.
The exam papers were marked incorrectly.

5 Complete the sentences with *by* or *with*.

1 Your boots are covered _____*with*_____ mud!

2 The room was decorated _____*with*_____ colourful balloons.

3 Microwave cooking was discovered _____*by*_____ accident.

4 The jewellery was made _____*with*_____ recycled plastic.

5 Was the bad connection caused _____*by*_____ a damaged cable?

6 When blue is mixed _____*with*_____ red paint, you get purple.

7 Hamlet was written _____*by*_____ Shakespeare.

8 The WiFi was fixed _____*by*_____ an engineer.

6 Choose the correct option to complete the sentences.

1 Our dog is *took* / *taken* for a walk twice a day.

2 The electric fridge *was* / *were* invented by Florence Parpart.

3 Food that *aren't* / *isn't* processed is much healthier for you.

4 Their passports *are* / *were* stolen on the way to the airport, so they couldn't catch their flight.

5 The equipment was checked carefully *by* / *with* the diving instructor.

6 The film was *shown* / *showed* in an outdoor cinema.

7 Her desk was covered *with* / *by* books and pieces of paper.

8 That house was designed *with* / *by* Gaudí.

7 Tick the correct sentences. Then correct the mistakes.

1 Is the patients looked after well by the nurses?

Are the patients looked after well by the nurses?

2 The bikes in the garage are covered by dirt.

The bikes in the garage are covered with dirt.

3 They were spoke to so rudely by the waiter that they made a complaint.

They were spoken to so rudely by the waiter that they made a complaint.

4 All her flowers and vegetables were destroyed with the storm.

All her flowers and vegetables were destroyed by the storm.

5 I was given a car by my parents when I started university.

✔

6 New laptops were bought to the students.

New laptops were bought for the students.

7 Tina applied for the job and was interviewed by the manager on Friday.

✔

8 A big prize was awarded the creators of the invention.

A big prize was awarded to the creators of the invention.

Vocabulary

Prepositions

8 Complete the phrases with these prepositions.

| for (x2)   in (x2)   on   to (x2)   with (x3) |

1 be an expert ____*in*____ something

2 chat ____*with*____ someone

3 click ____*on*____ something

4 communicate ____*with*____ someone / something

5 have access ____*to*____ something

6 keep in touch ____*with*____ someone

7 look ____*for*____ something / someone

8 sign up ____*for*____ something

9 succeed ____*in*____ something

10 upload something ____*to*____ somewhere

9 Complete the sentences with the correct form of the prepositional phrases from Exercise 8.

1 I've ____*uploaded*____ some photos _____*to*_____ my new website. It took ages!

2 He ____*clicked on*____ a link he was sent, then he realised the link contained a virus.

3 The scientists ___*had / have access to*___ the biggest lab in the building.

4 She isn't very good at ___*keeping in touch with*___ her friends and family. She always forgets to call them.

5 Do you think we ___*communicate with*___ each other better with or without technology?

6 He entered the technology competition and ____*succeeded in*____ winning first prize.

7 The engineers ___*are / were experts in*___ robotics.

8 They've ____*signed up for*____ an online graphic design course.

9 In the evening, my sister probably spends two hours ____*chatting with*____ her friends on social media.

10 I wish I knew what my old college friend was doing now – I might try and _____*look for*_____ her online.

Exam practice

Open cloze

10 **For each question, write the correct answer. Write one word for each gap.**

1 The new equipment _____was_____ not delivered yesterday.

2 This device _____is_____ used for tracking your movement. It's tracking it right now!

3 Was the first satellite invented _____by_____ a Russian?

4 I spilled my drink and my phone was covered _____with_____ water.

5 The machines _____are_____ powered with solar energy.

6 Special prizes were given _____to_____ the best science projects.

7 Tablets were bought _____for_____ the children.

8 We _____were_____ told not to stay up late as we had school the following day.

Multiple-choice cloze

11 **For each question, choose the correct answer.**

1 I can hear you, but I can't see you – your ___ isn't working.

  A mouse   **B** battery   **C** webcam   **D** WiFi

2 He couldn't decide if he should buy a tablet instead ___ a laptop.

  A for   **B** than   **C** with   **D** of

3 Look at the weather ___ – the next few days are going to be miserable!

  A forecast   **B** newscast   **C** overcast   **D** broadcast

4 You just need to click and ___ the photo to this box here, and then press 'enter'.

  A pull   **B** drag   **C** open   **D** push

5 The testing lab was broken ___ by some angry protestors.

  A onto   **B** across   **C** around   **D** into

6 Some ___ was updated on my computer last night.

  A connection   **B** software   **C** printer   **D** device

7 Could you pass me the remote ___ , please?

  A power   **B** energy   **C** control   **D** server

8 Oh no! I think my laptop has just ___ again!

  A crashed   **B** smashed   **C** hit   **D** knocked

Speaking

12 **Work in pairs. Discuss the questions.**

- What's your favourite gadget used for?
- What do you think is the best invention so far?
- If you could invent something, what would it be?
- Is technology used safely by everyone?
- Is it better to communicate with social media or face to face?

Unit 18

Awareness

1 **Which of these sentences are correct (C) and incorrect (I)?**

1 A new satellite is been launched today. __I__
2 The science fair has been held in the town for years. __C__
3 Batteries should to be stored in a cool, dry place. __I__
4 Safety glasses must be worn in this area. __C__
5 Inventors ought be well paid for their work. __I__
6 After the bike had been repaired, I sold it. __C__
7 Personal identification has to be showed. __I__
8 Applications for the job need to be sent by 10th June. __C__
9 All the exams will been corrected by the end of today. __I__
10 His phone can't be lost – he's just called me. __C__

How many did you get right? ☐

Grammar

Passive sentences with modals

To use a modal verb in a passive sentence, we use the modal verb + *be* + past participle. The verb *be* does not change.
*Old devices **can be reused** or **recycled**.*
*The computer **should be switched off** when not in use.*
*The lab doors **must be locked** at night.*

The passive: other tenses

In other tenses, the verb *be* in the passive sentence is in the same tense as the main verb in the active sentence. It is followed by the past participle of the main verb.

Tense	Active	Passive
present simple	take / takes	am /are / is taken
present continuous	am / are / is taking	am /are / is being taken
past simple	took	was / were taken
past continuous	was / were taking	was / were being taken
present perfect simple	have / has taken	have / has been taken
past perfect simple	had taken	had been taken
future simple	will take	will be taken

Note

There is no passive form for the future continuous, present perfect continuous or past perfect continuous.

Grammar exercises

2 **Read the sentences and underline the passive forms.**

1 The computer program should be finished by the developers today.
2 The online competition will be entered by several students.
3 Calming music can be used if it's difficult for you to fall asleep.
4 Your answers ought to be corrected.
5 The new smartphone is being sold everywhere.
6 I went to the café while my bike was being fixed.
7 Her new album has just been released.
8 The lab equipment will need to be put away safely.

3 Choose the correct option to complete the sentences.

1 Can audiobooks *be downloaded* / *being downloaded* from the internet easily?

2 This recipe hasn't *been written* / *be written* very clearly – I don't understand what I need to do.

3 We *have been taken* / *are being taken* to the museum by the school. We're going by coach.

4 Your homework must *be done* / *to be done* by the time I get home.

5 The competition winner can't *be chosen* / *been chosen* until tomorrow.

6 The scientists' work *was celebrated* / *has been celebrated* with a big party last night.

7 Sara's new tablet is *be delivered* / *being delivered* today – she's really looking forward to using it.

8 Your laptop should *be checked* / *to be checked* for viruses.

4 Match the beginnings of the sentences (1–8) with their endings (a–h).

1 The alarm batteries should — `c`   a be connected to the internet.

2 My computer can't — `a`   b be broadcast in the summer.

3 The final design had to — `d`   c be replaced every six months.

4 My laptop is — `g`   d be handed in yesterday.

5 That message shouldn't — `h`   e been viewed by thousands of people.

6 The video on social media has — `e`   f be deleted. They contain personal information.

7 Those files ought to — `f`   g being repaired at the moment.

8 His new TV show will — `b`   h be sent; it's unkind.

5 Choose the correct option (a–b) to complete the sentences.

1 You ___ around the city by a guide if you want, but it's expensive.

  a are being driven   **(b)** can be driven

2 Endangered animals ___ to help save our wildlife.

  a haven't been protected   **(b)** have to be protected

3 He ___ for the job as he doesn't have enough experience.

  a needn't be selected   **(b)** shouldn't be selected

4 Power stations must ___ for safety reasons.

  (a) be carefully monitored   **b** to be carefully monitored

5 These songs ought to ___ ; they're amazing!

  (a) be recorded   **b** being recorded

6 I wish his message ___ more clearly.

  (a) had been communicated   **b** has been communicated

7 The data ___ on the website.

  (a) won't be saved   **b** be saved

8 The screen needs ___ with a special liquid.

  a be cleaned   **(b)** to be cleaned

6 Rewrite the sentences in the passive.

1 Can you use this device to record videos?
Can this device be used to record videos?

2 A virus can destroy a computer system.
A computer system can be destroyed by a virus.

3 You should finish your homework before you play computer games.
Your homework should be finished before you play computer games.

4 We mustn't accidentally delete this document.
The document mustn't be accidentally deleted.

5 You needn't draw your design by hand; you could use some design software.
Your design needn't be drawn by hand; some design software could be used.

6 You have to request permission from the scientist before you use the lab.
Permission from the scientist has to be requested before the lab is used.

7 They ought to buy more equipment for the classrooms.
More equipment ought to be bought for the classrooms.

8 You must record your results after finishing the experiment.
Your results must be recorded after finishing the experiment.

Sentence transformation

7 Complete the second sentence so that it has a similar meaning to the first sentence, using the word given.
Do not change the word given. You must use between two and five words.

1 Someone has smashed the tablet screen.
The tablet screen _____ _has been_ _____ smashed. **BEEN**

2 The cat should be taken to the vet because it isn't well.
The cat _____ _ought to be_ _____ taken to the vet because it isn't well. **TO**

3 They should order new office furniture; what we've got now is very old.
New office furniture _____ _needs to be ordered_ _____ ; what we've got now is very old. **NEEDS**

4 A pedestrian had been hit by a car, so someone called an ambulance.
An _____ _ambulance was called_ _____ because a pedestrian had been hit by a car. **WAS**

5 The songs were downloading onto my phone while I was watching a film.
The songs _were being downloaded_ onto my phone while I was watching a film. **BEING**

6 The engineer will have fixed the internet connection by the end of the day.
The internet connection _will have been fixed by_ the engineer by the end of the day. **BY**

7 There might be books all over her desk; she isn't very tidy.
Her desk _might be covered with_ books; she isn't very tidy. **COVERED**

8 He didn't buy the software separately – it was already installed onto the laptop.
The software _wasn't / was not sold_ separately – it was already installed onto the laptop. **SOLD**

Vocabulary

Collocations and expressions

8 Complete the collocations and expressions with these words.

be	carry out	data	easy	make	personal	signals	track	value	waste

1 be good ___value___
2 be ___easy___ to use
3 be a ___waste___ of time
4 collect ___data___
5 send ___signals___ to

6 ___make___ a video call
7 ___carry out___ someone's instructions
8 keep ___track___ of
9 give ___personal___ information
10 ___be___ yourself

9 Complete the sentences with the correct form of the collocations and expressions from Exercise 8.

1 Satellites receive and ___send signals to___ different places on Earth.
2 You mustn't ___give personal information___ to anyone you don't know or trust.
3 My brother thinks playing video games ___is a waste of time___ .
4 It's very difficult to ___keep track of___ time when you're having so much fun.
5 This laptop has been reduced in price – I think it ___'s / is good value___ .
6 Julia had ___been making video calls___ all day long and was tired of looking at her screen.
7 Big technology companies are constantly ___collecting data___ about us.
8 This tablet is really ___easy to use___ .
9 Don't copy what everyone is doing; you should always ___be yourself___ .
10 Please listen to what I'm saying, as you must ___carry out___ my instructions carefully.

Exam practice

Open cloze

10 For each question, write the correct answer. Write one word for each gap.

1 My smartphone is ___being___ repaired today – the screen is broken.
2 He couldn't work ___out___ how his webcam had been broken; he'd been very careful with it.
3 The best invention award ___will___ be given to the winner tomorrow.
4 This website is aimed ___at___ teenagers who love music.
5 The man who stole her laptop ___has___ been found and is at the police station.
6 These products have been made ___by___ a 3D printer.
7 Toys from home ___must___ not be taken into school, as the children will lose them.
8 Our house needs ___to___ be rented this summer, as we'll be living aboard.

18

Multiple-choice cloze

11 **For each question, choose the correct answer.**

1 When he gets lost, he uses the map __ his phone.

   A in **B** with **C** for **(D)** on

2 We're working on a project and need to __ information on how people use the internet in different countries.

   A store **(B)** gather **C** take **D** stores

3 You must be __ when you shop online. Some websites are not what they say they are.

   A honest **(B)** careful **C** yourself **D** precise

4 She's very kind and really __ other people's feelings.

   (A) respects **B** carries **C** tests **D** succeeds

5 If satellites get lost in space, they could __ other spacecraft.

   A protect **B** repair **(C)** endanger **D** communicate

6 The rules on this building site must be followed to ensure your __ at all times.

   A education **(B)** safety **C** communication **D** emergency

7 At school we have a big __ room for technology education.

   A laptop **(B)** computer **C** lab **D** control

8 Electric cars are better __ the environment only if the electricity they use is clean and sustainable.

   A to **B** with **(C)** for **D** about

Writing

12 **Read the writing task and write your answer in about 100 words. Try to present your ideas in order using linking expressions.**

Write an opinion essay about this statement:
Schools should spend more time teaching science, technology, engineering and maths, and less time teaching subjects like history and geography.

Unit 19

Awareness

1 **Which of these sentences are correct (C) and incorrect (I)?**

1 Todd said that he was watching a documentary. _C_

2 Araf said that he had been reading Melville's novel Moby Dick. _C_

3 Lyle told that the singer was getting married. _I_

4 My teacher said that she can play five musical instruments. _I_

5 Nancy said that she's doing ballet. _I_

6 He said that they're going to get concert tickets. _I_

7 Henrik and Jacob said they had been listening to music all day. _C_

8 She said that we ought to take drama lessons. _C_

9 Iraj said he will watch the new comedy show. _I_

10 Ellie said that her favourite music was jazz. _C_

How many did you get right? ☐

Grammar

Reported speech: statements

We can report the exact words someone said using quotation marks. This is called 'direct speech'.
Emilia said, 'I'm at the Louvre Museum in Paris!'

We can also report the general idea of what someone said. This is called 'reported speech'.
*Emilia said **that she was** at the Louvre Museum in Paris.*

When we report what someone said in the past:

• we change present verb forms to past verb forms, e.g. present simple to past simple.
'I'm an actor.' → *He said that **he was** an actor.*

• we often use **that** before the reported words.
'I like documentaries.' → *She said **that** she liked documentaries.*

• we change the pronouns in the reported words.
*'**We** often go to concerts.'* → ***They** said that **they** often went to concerts.*

In reported speech, we usually change the verb used by the speaker by putting it back one tense.

Direct speech	Reported speech
present simple	**past simple**
'She **likes** pop music,' he said.	He said (that) she **liked** pop music.
present continuous	**past continuous**
'She **is playing** her new video game,' he said.	He said (that) **she was** playing her new video game.
present perfect simple	**past perfect simple**
'They **have bought** a new laptop,' she said.	She said (that) they **had bought** a new laptop.
present perfect continuous	**past perfect continuous**
'They **have been practising** all week,' she said.	She said (that) they **had been practising** all week.
past simple	**past perfect simple**
'He **watched** a documentary,' she said.	She said (that) he **had watched** a documentary.
past continuous	**past perfect continuous**
'He **was writing** about a new band,' she said.	She said (that) he **had been writing** about a new band.

Other changes in verb forms are as follows:

can	could
'Ben **can** play the guitar,' she said.	She said (that) Ben **could** play the guitar.
may	might
'He **may** come to the cinema,' she said.	She said (that) he **might** come to the cinema.
must	had to
'He **must** pay for the tickets later,' she said.	She said (that) he **had to** pay for the tickets later.
will	would
'They **will** never like classical music,' she said.	She said (that) they **would** never like classical music.

Note

1 We can leave out *that*.

They said that they had read the book before.
They said they had read the book before.

2 The following tenses and words do not change in reported speech: past perfect simple, past perfect continuous, *would, could, should, ought to, used to, mustn't* and *must* when it refers to certainty (not obligation or necessity).

say and *tell*

We often use the verbs *say* and *tell* in reported speech. We follow *tell* with an object.
*The actor **said** they would love her new film.*
*The actor **told her friends** they would love her new film.*

Grammar exercises

2 **Rewrite the sentences in reported speech.**

1 'I'll get the concert tickets,' Layla said.

Layla said *(that) she would get the concert tickets* .

2 'The lead singer is leaving the band,' Tom said.

Tom said *(that) the lead singer was leaving the band* .

3 'He can borrow a violin from school,' she said.

She said *(that) he could borrow a violin from school* .

4 'We had fun at the cinema,' they said.

They said *(that) they had had fun at the cinema* .

5 'Dad doesn't like watching TV,' we said.

We said *(that) Dad didn't like watching TV* .

6 'The children will have parts in the school play,' Gillian said.

Gillian said *(that) the children would have parts in the school play* .

7 'I have to record some songs,' Max said.

Max said *(that) he had to record some songs* .

8 'I've been to the Sydney Opera House,' my aunt said.

My aunt said *(that) she had been to the Sydney Opera House* .

3 Julia went on a class trip to an acting school last week and met some of the students and teachers. Report what they told Julia.

1 I have learned how to perform confidently. (Jake)

Jake said (that) he had learned / learnt how to perform confidently.

2 There are three film studios. (Mr Francis)

Mr Francis said (that) there were three film studios.

3 I'm struggling to remember all the lines for the play. (Adele)

Adele said (that) she was struggling to remember all the lines for the play.

4 I'll be happy if I become a professional actor. (Pavel)

Pavel said (that) he would be happy if he became a professional actor.

5 We're putting on a huge show. (Ms Drake)

Ms Drake said (that) they were putting on a huge show.

6 I've been busy making costumes and accessories. (Theo)

Theo said (that) he had been busy making costumes and accessories.

7 I'm doing some voice training. (Mia)

Mia said (that) she was doing some voice training.

8 I may go back to the school in the future. (Freya)

Freya said (that) she might go back to the school in the future.

4 Match the beginnings of the sentences (1–8) with their endings (a–h).

1 Luca told me he had just   *c*   **a** Elvis Presley's Graceland one day.

2 Elin said she would visit   *a*   **b** switch off the TV and go to bed.

3 Dan said he was tired because he   *f*   **c** flown back from Italy.

4 Eva told her parents she wanted   *e*   **d** some magic tricks.

5 Michel told his sister that she ought to   *b*   **e** to enter a talent show.

6 Jo said she was relaxing and   *h*   **f** had been practising with his band all evening.

7 Laura said she might learn   *d*   **g** feeling well and that she wanted to go home.

8 Clare told us she wasn't   *g*   **h** listening to an interesting podcast.

5 Complete the sentences with the correct form of *say* or *tell*.

1 Tina _____*told*_____ me that she was enjoying her drama course.

2 James _____*said*_____ that he needed some new drums.

3 'I'll take you to the show,' Bridget _____*told*_____ me.

4 Hans _____*said*_____ he was surprised that he had got a part in the show.

5 Yuko _____*told*_____ us that she was going to see *Madame Butterfly* at the opera house.

6 The celebrity _____*told*_____ the photographer to stop following him.

7 'Meet me at the theatre,' he _____*told*_____ them.

8 The actor _____*said*_____ that she needed to take a break.

6 Choose the correct option to complete the sentences. Then write what the speakers said in direct speech.

1 Kieron told me he (wouldn't) / will sing the song.
   'I won't sing the song.'

2 She said that the main actor had (been feeling) / felt nervous all day.
   'The main actor has been feeling nervous all day.'

3 Vince said he would (see) / saw everyone at drama club.
   'I'll see everyone at drama club.'

4 They said they (were) / are going to arrive on time.
   'We're going to arrive on time.'

5 He said I (should) / ought go to the concert in the park.
   'You should go to the concert in the park.'

6 They said that they are going to / (would) take part in the show.
   'We'll take part in the show.'

7 Mary said she (had to) / must talk to the manager.
   'I have to / must talk to the manager.'

8 Dean said that he (had been) / has been up all night learning the lines for the play.
   'I've been up all night learning the lines for the play.'

7 Rewrite the sentences in reported speech.

1 Toby said, 'You ought to practise more often.'
   Toby said (that) I / we ought to practise more often.

2 Billy said, 'The new comedy show is very funny.'
   Billy said (that) the new comedy show was very funny.

3 'I'm writing a new book,' she said.
   She said (that) she was writing a new book.

4 'I got the main part in the play,' he told them.
   He told them (that) he had got the main part in the play.

5 'I can't afford to buy tickets for the opera,' he said.
   He said (that) he couldn't afford to buy tickets for the opera.

6 'It's a very famous theatre,' the tour guide told us.
   The tour guide told us (that) it was a very famous theatre.

7 'I don't like that actor,' said Mark.
   Mark said (that) he didn't like that actor.

8 'We may be a bit late for the show,' Pete said.
   Pete said (that) they might be a bit late for the show.

9 'You should be more polite to the author,' he told them.
   He told them (that) they should be more polite to the author.

10 'Those are the dancers in the ballet,' my friend told me.
   My friend told me / said (that) those were the dancers in the ballet.

Vocabulary

Phrasal verbs

8 Choose the correct option (a–b).

1 *turn into*
   (a) change into someone or something different
   b perform

2 *get on with*
   a write something
   (b) start or continue doing something

3 *turn down*
   a relax / have a rest
   (b) make something quieter

4 *turn off*
   a stop doing something
   (b) finish something by moving a switch or button

5 *put off*
   (a) delay an event or activity until later
   b dislike something

6 *turn out*
   (a) be discovered to be / prove to be
   b leave

7 *fill in*
   a grow
   (b) complete

8 *turn on*
   (a) start something by moving a switch or button
   b become popular

9 *be into*
   a let someone into a place
   (b) be very interested and involved in something

10 *turn up*
   (a) make something louder
   b create something

9 Complete the sentences with the correct form of the phrasal verbs from Exercise 8.

1 She said that the play had ____*turned out*____ to be much better than she thought it would.

2 He said that we ought to ____*get on with*____ the class project, even though it was the weekend.

3 He ____*filled in*____ his bank details and made the payment.

4 The weather forecast was terrible, so they ____*put off*____ the outdoor concert until the weather got better.

5 She told me to ____*turn up*____ the radio because she loved the song that was playing.

6 He had loved music since he was a child and he ____*turned into*____ a very skilled guitarist.

7 All my friends ____*are into*____ pop music, but I much prefer jazz.

8 He said he had forgotten to ____*turn off*____ his phone when he was at the cinema, and the person behind him got annoyed.

9 'Don't ____*turn on*____ the TV; I'm trying to learn my lines,' she told her brother.

10 Would you please ____*turn down*____ your music? I can hear it through your headphones!

Exam practice

Open cloze

10 For each question, write the correct answer. Write one word for each gap.

1 Ben said ____*that*____ he had never seen a better film.

2 Tim ____*told*____ me that he would come and take me to the show.

3 My parents said they ____*could*____ not buy theatre tickets for Saturday night as there were none left.

4 Trudy said she might ____*be*____ trying out a new ballet class, but she wasn't sure.

5 She told me that she ____*had*____ made the costumes for the show because no one else was able to do it.

6 He said that Steve had ____*gone*____ to a festival for the weekend, and would be back on Monday.

7 James told me that the tickets ____*were*____ there on the shelf.

8 Gina said that she ____*would*____ definitely go to Hollywood one day.

19

11 **For each question, choose the correct answer.**

1 My grandad loves this ___ show even though he gets most of the answers wrong.

   A talent   **(B)** quiz   **C** documentary   **D** chat

2 At the end of the concert, everyone in the audience stood up to ___ loudly.

   (A) clap   **B** play   **C** dance   **D** perform

3 I bought a second-hand violin, which was in very good ___ .

   A repair   **B** fix   **C** state   **(D)** condition

4 Let's go to the ticket ___ to see if we can get some cheap seats.

   A place   **(B)** office   **C** box   **D** room

5 I was sorry when the film was ___ . I didn't want it to end!

   A under   **(B)** over   **C** up   **D** around

6 What a strange story. I didn't expect the main character to end ___ getting lost in the jungle.

   A out   **B** with   **(C)** up   **D** on

7 Unless you become a big movie star, it isn't very easy to ___ a lot of money as an actor.

   (A) make   **B** do   **C** create   **D** take

8 She sang all the songs ___ ; her performance was the best I've seen.

   A quickly   **B** softly   **C** carefully   **(D)** perfectly

Speaking

12 **Work in pairs. Discuss the questions, then report what your partner said.**

- Is music important to you? Why / Why not?
- What was the last concert you went to? Did you enjoy it?
- How often do you watch films? What films do you like?
- Do you have any actors that you particularly like or dislike? Why?
- What kind of things do you like reading?

1 **Which of these sentences are correct (C) and incorrect (I)?**

1 Nina said that she was practising the piano now. ___I___

2 'When did you record your first song?' she asked. ___C___

3 They asked me when did I make my first film. ___I___

4 They asked do I like classical music. ___I___

5 He said they were going to the cinema that day. ___C___

6 Greg asked her if she had written the song. ___C___

7 He asked me if I could clean up the studio. ___C___

8 'What time does the play start,' he asked? ___I___

9 'Don't play the music loudly,' he told his son. ___C___

10 She asked we could take her to the concert. ___I___

How many did you get right? ☐

Grammar

Reported speech: changes to pronouns, possessives, time and place

Remember to change pronouns where necessary.
'**We** are going to perform in a concert.' → She said (that) **they** were going to perform in a concert.

We also change possessive adjectives.
'Those are **my** ballet shoes.' → He said that those were **his** ballet shoes.

There are often changes in words that show time and place too.

now	then
'I'm playing the saxophone **now**,' she said.	She said she was playing the saxophone **then**.
today	that day
'We're going to the concert **today**,' he said.	He said they were going to the concert **that day**.
tonight	that night
'They can go to the performance **tonight**,' she said.	She said they could go to the performance **that night**.
yesterday	the previous day / the day before
'I saw them play **yesterday**,' she said.	She said she had seen them play **the previous day / the day before**.
last week / month	the previous week / month / the week / month before
'He recorded the album **last month**,' she said.	She said he had recorded the album **the previous month / the month before**.
tomorrow	the next day / the following day
'I'll get the costumes **tomorrow**,' she said.	She said she would get the costumes **the next day / the following day**.
next week / month	the following week / month
'We're going to the festival **next weekend**,' she said.	She said they were going to the festival **the following weekend**.
this / these	that / those
'**This** is my guitar,' she said.	She said **that** was her guitar.
ago	before
'I bought that magazine two weeks **ago**,' she said.	She said she had bought that magazine two weeks **before**.
at the moment	at that moment
'He's playing in an orchestra **at the moment**,' she said.	She said he was playing in an orchestra **at that moment**.
here	there
'Your keys are **here** on the table,' she said.	She said my keys were **there** on the table.

20

Reported speech: questions

When we report questions, changes in tenses, pronouns, possessive adjectives, time and place are the same as in reported statements. In reported questions, the verb follows the subject as in ordinary statements and we do not use question marks.

When a direct question has a question word, we use this word in the reported question.
'**When** did you start writing poetry?' he asked.
He asked **when** I had started writing poetry.

When a direct question does not have a question word, we use *if* or *whether* in the reported question.
'Do you like going to the theatre?' he asked.
He asked **if / whether** I liked going to the theatre.

Grammar exercises

2 **Complete the reported statements with pronouns and possessive adjectives.**

1 Ana said, 'I want to go to the cinema with my friends.'
   Ana said that she wanted to go to the cinema with _____ *her* _____ friends.

2 'We're taking our parents to the classical music concert,' they said.
   They said they were taking _____ *their* _____ parents to the classical music concert.

3 Tom said, 'I have to get some flowers for my sister, the star of the show!'
   Tom said that _____ *he* _____ had to get some flowers for _____ *his* _____ sister, the star of the show.

4 Peter said, 'I'll meet you this morning at the art college.'
   Peter said that he would meet _____ *me* _____ that morning at the art college.

5 Freya and Adia said, 'We've lost our theatre tickets.'
   Freya and Adia said that _____ *they* _____ had lost _____ *their* _____ theatre tickets.

6 Ella told me, 'I can't perform in your play tonight.'
   Ella said that _____ *she* _____ couldn't perform in _____ *my* _____ play that night.

7 'We're going to write our own opera,' Billy and Nat said.
   Billy and Nat said that _____ *they* _____ were going to write _____ *their* _____ own opera.

8 Suzy said 'We'll celebrate my sister's birthday at the weekend.
   Suzy said _____ *they* _____ would celebrate _____ *her* _____ sister's birthday at the weekend.

9 Jules and Jim said, 'We had an awful time at the dance class and we have hurt our feet!'
   Jules and Jim said _____ *they* _____ had had an awful time at the dance class and that _____ *they* _____ had hurt _____ *their* _____ feet.

10 'I was watching a film when my TV suddenly turned off,' said Daniel.
   Daniel said _____ *he* _____ had been watching a film when _____ *his* _____ TV had suddenly turned off.

3 Choose the correct option to complete the sentences. Then write what the speakers said in direct speech.

1 Lorna said she was going to see the new horror film (that night)/ tonight.
 'I'm going to see the new horror film tonight.'

2 They said they were watching a talent show *at the moment* / at that moment.
 'We're watching a talent show at the moment.'

3 Henry told me he would sign up for singing lessons *next* / the following week.
 'I'll sign up for singing lessons next week.'

4 She told me that my violin was there / *here* on the shelf.
 'Your violin is here on the shelf.'

5 He said he had bought the concert tickets *last* / the previous month.
 'I bought the concert tickets last month.'

6 We said we would finish the song the next day / *tomorrow*.
 'We'll finish the song tomorrow.'

7 Leo said *this* / that was the best he could do.
 'This is the best I can do.'

8 Julia said she was playing the clarinet then / *now*.
 'I'm playing the clarinet now.'

4 Rewrite the questions in reported speech.

1 'How old is your sister?' she asked me.
 She asked me how old my sister was.

2 He asked, 'Who's that man?'
 He asked who that man was.

3 'Where are your headphones?' she asked me.
 She asked me where my headphones were.

4 'When should we go to the cinema?' she asked Tim.
 She asked Tim when they should go to the cinema.

5 'Can you play the saxophone?' Clem asked the students.
 Clem asked the students if / whether they could play the saxophone.

6 'What have you done this morning?' my friend asked us.
 My friend asked us what we had done that morning.

7 'Did you go to the concert last weekend?' he asked her.
 He asked her if / whether she had gone to the concert the previous weekend.

8 He asked, 'Whose books are these?'
 He asked whose books those were.

5 Last week a journalist, Lara, interviewed local pop singer May Lavin about her career. Complete Lara's questions in reported speech.

1 'When did you realise you wanted to be a pop singer?'
Lara asked May _when she realised (that) she had wanted to be a pop singer_ .

2 'Where did you have your first concert?'
Lara asked May _where she had had her first concert_ .

3 'How many albums have you made?'
Lara asked May _how many albums she had made_ .

4 'Are your songs about real-life experiences?'
Lara asked May _if / whether her songs were about real-life experiences_ .

5 'What do you dislike about the music business?'
Lara asked May _what she disliked about the music business_ .

6 'Are you planning to go on tour next year?'
Lara asked May _if / whether she was planning to go on tour the following year_ .

6 Rewrite the direct speech into reported speech and the reported speech into direct speech.

1 'What are your plans for the future?' she asked me.
She asked me _what my plans for the future were._

2 Jo said she hadn't stolen headphones from that shop.
Jo said, _'I didn't steal headphones from this shop.'_

3 Lee told us that he might be chosen for the school band; he would know the following week.
Lee told us, _'I may be chosen for the school band; I will know next week.'_

4 'Can you turn off this terrible show?' Mum asked Beth.
Mum asked Beth _if / whether she could turn off that terrible show._

5 'You must remember to take your guitar to practice today,' Ms Marks told Eva.
Ms Marks told Eva _(that) she had to remember to take her guitar to practice that day._

6 She asked her best friend if she could download some songs for her that night.
She asked her best friend, _'Can you download some songs for me tonight?'_

7 The manager told the musician he didn't need leave his hotel until the following day.
'You don't need to leave your hotel until tomorrow.' the manager told the musician.

8 'I really enjoy your music,' he told Eliza.
He told Eliza _(that) he really enjoyed her music._

9 Julia told her friend that she would take lots of photos.
'I'll take lots of photos.' Julia told her friend.

10 'I don't think you should do any dancing at the moment,' Trish told me.
Trish told me _(that) she didn't think I should do any dancing at that moment.'_

Sentence transformation

7 Complete the second sentence so that it has a similar meaning to the first sentence, using the word given. Do not change the word given. You must use between two and five words.

1 She said, 'It's been a long time since I had such fun.'
She said she had not _____ *had such fun for* _____ a long time. **FOR**

2 They wanted to know what time the ballet started.
'What time _____ *does the ballet start* _____?' they asked. **START**

3 'We must leave now, or we will miss the start of the show,' said Anya.
Anya said that we _____ *had to leave then* _____ or we would miss the start of the show. **HAD**

4 'Can you drive me to the performance, please, Dad?'
I _____ *asked Dad if he could* _____ drive me to the performance **IF**

5 The actor said he would think about that.
'I _____ *will think about it* _____,' said the actor. **IT**

6 My cousins said 'We are going camping next week and can't wait!'
My cousins said that _____ *they were going camping the* _____ following week and they couldn't wait. **THE**

7 'Can you lend Kate your guitar until tomorrow?' his sister asked.
His sister asked whether Kate _____ *could borrow his* _____ guitar until the next day. **BORROW**

8 'I should take Mina to the play for her birthday,' Steve said.
Steve said _____ *he ought to take* _____ Mina to the play for her birthday. **TO**

Vocabulary

Word formation

8 Complete the table.

Noun	Verb	Adjective	Adverb
acting / [1] _____ *actor* _____	act	active	actively
[2] _____ *drama* _____	dramatise	dramatic	dramatically
entertainment / entertainer	[3] _____ *entertain* _____	entertaining / entertained	entertainingly
[4] _____ *equipment* _____	equip	equipped	–
modernisation	modernise	[5] _____ *modern* _____	–
music / [6] _____ *musician* _____ / musical	–	musical	musically
performance / performer	[7] _____ *perform* _____	performing	–
thrill / [8] _____ *thriller* _____	thrill	thrilling / thrilled	thrillingly

9 Complete the sentences with words from Exercise 8.

1 He's reading a _____ *thriller* _____ at the moment; he can't put the book down.

2 Her parents aren't interested in _____ *modern* _____ music; they like songs from the 1990s!

3 They come from a very _____ *musical* _____ family – they all play at least two instruments.

4 More than fifty trucks of _____ *equipment* _____ were needed to put on the band's concert each night.

5 My best friend loves watching comedy series, but I prefer watching something more serious, like a good _____ *drama* _____.

6 Have you seen who the main _____ *performer* _____ is at the show on Saturday night?

7 These days, phones are used more for general _____ *entertainment* _____ than to make calls.

8 Before he began his _____ *acting* _____ career, he worked as a waiter in a Hollywood café.

20

Exam practice

Open cloze

10 For each question, write the correct answer. Write one word for each gap.

   1 She said she was listening to a podcast at _____*that*_____ moment.

   2 He wishes he had learned how to play a _____*musical*_____ instrument.

   3 They said they had seen a great play the _____*previous*_____ month.

   4 Grandma's favourite thing to watch on TV is a soap _____*opera*_____ , which is on four days a week.

   5 He said he would make an appointment the _____*following*_____ week.

   6 The video was put on social media, and it soon _____*went*_____ viral, with over five millions views.

   7 She said the interview had been broadcast on TV all over the world the week _____*before*_____ .

   8 He works _____*as*_____ a photographer.

Multiple-choice cloze

11 For each question, choose the correct answer.

   1 A member of the ___ made so much noise during the performance that he was asked to leave.

     A public   **(B)** audience   **C** band   **D** club

   2 She was a brilliant musician and was respected ___ everyone in the music business.

     A for   **B** with   **(C)** by   **D** on

   3 The dancers walked ___ the stage and the lights turned on.

     A into   **(B)** onto   **C** through   **D** about

   4 Many ___ are only famous because they appeared on a TV show – they don't have a specific talent.

     A heroes   **B** performers   **(C)** celebrities   **D** actors

   5 He asked where the remote control was because he wanted to ___ channel.

     A move   **B** turn   **C** press   **(D)** change

   6 The ___ is the leader of an orchestra.

     A player   **B** presenter   **C** manager   **(D)** conductor

   7 At the end of play, the ___ came down.

     A shutter   **B** screen   **(C)** curtain   **D** scene

   8 These instruments are made ___ of recycled materials.

     (A) out   **B** by   **C** for   **D** with

Writing

12 Read the writing task and write your answer in about 100 words. Try to use words and phrases to show the order of events.

Your English teacher has asked you to write story. Your story must begin with this sentence:
The big school performance was about to start.

Grammar

1 Complete the sentences with the passive form of the verbs.

1 My laptop _____*was damaged*_____ (damage) when I spilled my coffee on it last week.

2 Our road _____*is being repaired*_____ (repair) right now.

3 Security cameras _____*are often installed*_____ (often install) in buildings to help prevent crime.

4 Today, many robotic pets _____*are designed / are being designed*_____ (design) by American companies.

5 By 2050, I believe spacecraft _____*will be created*_____ (create) by 3D printers that will take us on trips to the moon.

6 I hope that treatments for people who are seriously ill _____*will be found*_____ (find) soon.

7 Some very important data _____*is saved*_____ (save) on this computer – be careful not to delete any of it.

8 Cables which provide us with high-speed internet _____*were laid*_____ (lay) in my town last month.

2 Choose the correct option to complete the sentences.

1 My project *was* / *is* chosen to represent our school at the science museum last Friday.

2 The batteries for your headphones should *be* / *are* recharged about every six hours.

3 All the lights in the lab have *to be* / *been* turned off at the end of the day.

4 This cool little gadget *is* / *is being* used for a variety of purposes, especially for camping trips.

5 He was always *been* / *being* asked to stay after school to help in the library, and he really disliked it.

6 This year's gaming tournament *is played* / *will be played* at the new conference centre in town.

7 The builders *were* / *were being* hurt because they didn't have the proper clothing.

8 It wasn't until he got home that he realised his phone *was* / *had been* stolen.

3 Choose the correct option (a–b).

1 The teacher told them that they should always do their homework.
   a 'You should have always done your homework.'
   b 'You should always do your homework.'

2 The workers said the owner would visit the factory the following month.
   a 'The owner will visit the factory the following month.'
   b 'The owner will visit the factory next month.'

3 He said the accident had done a lot of damage to the equipment in his lab.
   a 'The accident has done a lot of damage to the equipment in my lab.'
   b 'The accident had done a lot of damage to the equipment in his lab.'

4 He said that the library might open a bit late that day.
   a 'The library may open a bit late today.'
   b 'The library was open a bit late today.'

5 Lyra told us that the new computers had been ordered the day before.
   a 'The new computers were ordered yesterday.'
   b 'The new computers had been ordered yesterday.'

6 She said that gadget was the most useful thing she had ever created.
   a 'This gadget is the most useful thing I have ever created.'
   b 'That gadget was the most useful thing I have ever created.'

4 Rewrite the sentences in reported speech.

1 'Can you do me a favour, please?' my sister asked me.

My sister asked me *if / whether I could do her a favour* .

2 'This is too much money to pay for theatre tickets,' Yoko said.

Yoko said that *that was too much money to pay for theatre tickets* .

3 'I'll be back from the party by eleven o'clock,' Julia said.

Julia said that *she would be back from the party by eleven o'clock* .

4 'You need to tidy up all these clothes!' Mum told me.

Mum told me that *I needed to tidy up all those / my clothes* .

5 'Your instruments are here on the table,' the music teacher told us.

The music teacher told us that *our instruments were there on the table* .

6 'Where is the art museum?' they asked the tour guide.

They asked the tour guide *where the art museum was* .

7 'I didn't delete all the files,' Jake said.

Jake said that *he hadn't deleted all the files* .

8 'Are you going to the jazz festival next weekend?' Ollie asked us.

Ollie asked *(us) if / whether we were going to the jazz festival the following weekend* .

5 Find one mistake in each sentence. Then correct the mistakes. Sometimes more than one answer is possible.

1 Cory said they had had an amazing time at the concert last weekend.

Cory said that they had had an amazing time at the concert the previous weekend / the weekend before.

2 Three houses were destroyed with the fire.

Three houses were destroyed by the fire.

3 Vince said his father doesn't like watching soap operas.

Vince said his father didn't like watching soap operas.

4 She said that she must come to the party, but she wasn't sure yet.

She said that she might come to the party, but she wasn't sure yet.

5 I'm given a gift by him the day before.

I was given a gift by him the day before.

6 They asked her she enjoyed listening to different kinds of music.

They asked her if / whether she enjoyed listening to different kinds of music.

7 After I baked a cake with the children, the kitchen floor was covered by flour.

After I baked a cake with the children, the kitchen floor was covered with flour.

8 My mother said me that I needed to do my homework.

My mother told me that I needed to do my homework.

6 Choose the correct option to complete the sentences.

1 Those photos *have* / *should* be downloaded to my laptop.
2 Our teacher told us we *were* / *are* going to the Louvre Museum *the next day* / *tomorrow*.
3 Can these clothes *be* / *are* given to the second-hand shop?
4 Peter said he *will* / *would* buy the concert tickets.
5 Jim asked us if we *can* / *could* meet him outside the cinema.
6 We'll be taught how to use the internet safely *with* / *by* the IT teacher.
7 Carlo said he *has to* / *had to* learn all his lines that night.
8 Dan said Mina *started* / *had started* cello lessons *last* / *the previous* year.
9 By 2090, we will *be eating* / *be eaten* 3D-printed food.
10 Mark said I *ought* / *should* to join the school band.

Use of English

Word formation

7 Use the word in the capitals to form a word that fits in the gap.

1 The ending of the series was really ___dramatic___ , wasn't it? — DRAMA
2 The school computer room was well ___equipped___ with new devices. — EQUIPMENT
3 Mum was ___thrilled___ with the flowers we gave her. — THRILL
4 They're planning to completely ___modernise___ the school library. — MODERN
5 Tickets are on sale for the new ___musical___ ; it's on at the New Theatre in August. — MUSIC
6 He loves watching all the talented street ___entertainers___ as he walks along the river. — ENTERTAIN
7 His uncle used to write plays and he is still very ___active___ in the theatre community. — ACT
8 She said that all the ___performers___ at the talent show had been amazing. — PERFORM

Open cloze

8 Complete the sentences with one word for each gap.

1 My brother is really ___into___ that TV show at the moment – he watches it every night.
2 'You have to choose the best singer,' the presenter said ___to___ the judges.
3 Mum said that trying to become a famous actor in Hollywood was a ___waste___ of time and that I should think about doing something different.
4 A lot of photos ___will___ be taken at the awards show tomorrow.
5 That song was written ___by___ my cousin.
6 They're ___being___ taught how to use different learning apps at school at the moment.
7 How do you keep in touch ___with___ all your family and friends?
8 My dad is an expert ___in___ jazz music.
9 She told me she just needed to ___make___ a video call, then she would finish work for the day.
10 I don't like folk music, but the concert turned ___out___ to be better than I thought it would.

Grammar

9 For questions 1–10, choose the word or phrase that best completes the sentence.

1 Modern technology ___ by billions of people.
- A   is using
- (B)   is used
- C   used
- D   was used

2 'I met a famous actor,' John ___ .
- (A)   told me
- B   said me
- C   told to me
- D   had told me

3 The burning building was filled ___ smoke.
- A   by
- (B)   with
- C   in
- D   out

4 Ted said that he was listening to some really cool music at ___ moment.
- A   a
- B   the
- C   this
- (D)   that

5 Will his second album ever ___ ?
- A   recorded
- (B)   be recorded
- C   recording
- D   have recorded

6 Dad asked me ___ I was tired.
- A   that
- B   what
- (C)   if
- D   so

7 Rowan said he ___ anyone at the lab that night.
- A   saw
- B   didn't see
- C   had seen
- (D)   hadn't seen

8 They said they ___ to come to my party.
- A   was able
- B   could
- (C)   weren't able
- D   couldn't

9 She said she would call me ___ following day.
- (A)   the
- B   this
- C   that
- D   a

10 The tourist asked us where the gallery ___ .
- A   has been
- B   is being
- C   is
- (D)   was

Vocabulary

10 For questions 11–20, choose the word or phrase that best completes the sentence.

11 The scientists need to do another ___ .
- A   software
- B   invention
- (C)   test
- D   equipment

12 The audience began ___ and cheering.
- A   practising
- (B)   clapping
- C   performing
- D   recording

13 Could you change ___ ? I don't like this show.
- A   player
- B   subject
- C   drama
- (D)   channel

14 You need to ___ the photo into this box here.
- A   chat
- (B)   drag
- C   click
- D   switch

15 The ___ was about space.
- (A)   documentary
- B   soap opera
- C   quiz show
- D   talent show

16 Oh no! I think my computer has ___ .
- (A)   crashed
- B   connected
- C   installed
- D   downloaded

17 Imagine life without access ___ the internet!
- A   with
- (B)   to
- C   by
- D   at

18 They need to ___ out the instructions carefully.
- A   design
- B   create
- C   develop
- (D)   carry

19 Use my tablet instead ___ your phone.
- (A)   of
- B   in
- C   on
- D   for

20 She asked if they could ___ down the music.
- A   fill
- (B)   turn
- C   run
- D   get

Unit 21

Awareness

1 **Which of these sentences are correct (C) and incorrect (I)?**

1 They weren't having their house painted last week. _____ C

2 Was Bill having his grass cut yesterday evening? _____ C

3 My best friend has had her wedding organised for her by a wedding planner. _____ C

4 Gina had her bag stolen a young girl at the weekend. _____ I

5 We have been had our neighbour's post delivered here since we moved in. _____ I

6 I'm checking my teeth at the dentist's. _____ I

7 The students will having their homework marked on Friday. _____ I

8 My sister and I getting our rooms decorated at the moment. _____ I

9 The school is having new computers installed in the classrooms next year. _____ C

10 We had a meal prepared for us at our table. _____ C

How many did you get right? [ ]

Grammar

The causative

We use the causative:

- to say that someone has arranged for somebody to do something for them.
*Siya **is having** her hair **cut** this afternoon.*

- to say that something unpleasant happened to someone.
*Mr Jones **has had** his window **broken**.*

We form the causative with *have* + object + past participle. It can be used in a variety of tenses.
*They **were having** their laptop **fixed** last week.*
*Uncle Frank **has been having** his suits **made** for him for years.*
*The school **has** its floors **cleaned** every night.*

> **Note**
> When we want to mention the agent, we use the word *by*.
> *He had his bookcase made **by a carpenter**.*

> **Note**
> We can also use *get* + object + past participle. This structure is less formal.
> *Paul **got** his phone **replaced** yesterday.*

Grammar exercises

2 **Tick the sentences that use the causative.**

1 Karen is painting her chest of drawers. [ ]

2 Tim wasn't having his car repaired. [✓]

3 Are they having security cameras installed? [✓]

4 Lena has been having her dress made for the wedding. [✓]

5 Henrik had been having his hair cut when he fell asleep. [✓]

6 The gardener had planted all his flowers. [ ]

7 The school will have all the classrooms cleaned during the weekend. [✓]

8 The little boy drew on the living room wall. [ ]

3 Choose the causative option to complete the sentences.

1 They *won't be having the school meals delivered* / *won't deliver the school meals* until next Monday.

2 Tom *had his bike checked* / *checked his bike* last night.

3 *A vet is examining my dog* / *I'm having my dog examined by a vet* at the moment.

4 Are the Morgans *having their kitchen designed by a professional* / *designing their kitchen*?

5 She *has her children looked after* / *looks after her children* every weekday.

6 Jake *will plant some trees* / *will have some trees planted* in his garden next month.

7 The dancers *have been having their costumes made* / *have been making their costumes* for the past few days.

8 He *had had his camera repaired* / *had repaired his camera* after he got back from summer holidays.

4 Complete the sentences with the causative form of the verbs.

1 _____*Have we had the pizzas delivered*_____ (we / the pizzas / deliver) yet? I'm hungry!

2 As soon as they _____*have had / got their flat painted*_____ (their flat / paint), they'll move in.

3 The school _____*had / got its website updated*_____ (its website / update) last Monday.

4 Tomorrow we _*are having / getting new software installed*_ (new software / install) on the office computers.

5 We _____*haven't had our essays marked*_____ (our essays / not / marked) by the teacher yet.

6 Mum and Dad _____*will have had the wall repaired*_____ (the wall / repair) by the end of the summer.

7 Freya _*is having / getting her hair washed and cut*_ (her hair / wash and cut) by the hairdreser tomorrow morning.

8 They _*were having / getting their heating fixed*_ (their heating / fix) when she called them last night.

5 Tick the correct sentences. Then correct the mistakes.

1 Ben had his bike stole from outside the school yesterday.
  Ben had his bike stolen from outside the school yesterday.

2 Lily is get her artwork exhibited at the local gallery at the moment.
  Lily is getting her artwork exhibited at the local gallery at the moment.

3 They were have the windows in the house replaced when it began to snow.
  They were having the windows in the house replaced when it began to snow.

4 Did Peter getting his dishwasher changed when you visited him?
  Was Peter getting his dishwasher changed when you visited him?

5 Tania had her shop windows broken last night.
  ✓

6 Bridget had her handbag stolen, so she went to the police station.
  ✓

7 My brother has his leg broken when he was hit by a car.
  My brother had his leg broken when he was hit by a car.

8 Teachers must get letters about the school trip send to the children's parents.
  Teachers must get letters about the school trip sent to the children's parents.

6 **Read about the people in the sentences and then answer the questions. Use the causative. Sometimes more than one answer is possible.**

1 The doctor is testing Billy's hearing. What is Billy doing?
   Billy is / He's having / getting his hearing tested (by the doctor).

2 This time tomorrow, a photographer will be taking the students' photos. What will the students be doing?
   The students / They will be having / getting their photos taken (by a photographer).

3 Dean's computer crashed, so his friend fixed it. What did Dean do?
   Dean / He had / got his computer fixed (by his friend).

4 If Sarah doesn't wear a helmet when she goes cycling, her parents will take her bike away from her. What will happen to her?
   Sarah / She will have her bike taken away from her (by her parents).

5 You fell during football practice and you hurt your knee. Your coach said a doctor must examine it. What must you do?
   I must have / get my knee examined (by a doctor).

6 Decorators were painting Lola's flat all day yesterday. What was she doing?
   She / Lola was having / getting her flat painted (by decorators) all day yesterday.

7 A window cleaner is cleaning our windows. What are we doing at the moment?
   We are having / getting our windows cleaned (by a window cleaner).

8 The assistant will send the head teacher's emails. What will the head teacher do?
   The head teacher will have / get his / her emails sent (by the assistant).

Sentence transformation

7 **Complete the second sentence so that it has a similar meaning to the first sentence, using the word given. Do not change the word given. You must use between two and five words.**

1 They arranged for their advert to be posted online last week.
   They _____ *had their advert posted* _____ online last week. **HAD**

2 Some metal tore my trousers this morning.
   I _____ *had my trousers torn by* _____ some metal this morning. **BY**

3 A man broke into my dad's van last night.
   My dad's van _____ *was broken into by* _____ a man last night. **WAS**

4 Someone is explaining the exercise to Stella.
   Stella _____ *is having / getting the exercise explained* _____ to her. **IS**

5 Vince pays a professional to clean his oven every six months.
   Vince _____ *gets his oven cleaned by* _____ a professional every six months. **GETS**

6 She has employed a decorator who will paint the rooms in her new flat.
   She _____ *'ll / will have the rooms painted* _____ in her new flat by a decorator. **HAVE**

7 Petra's arms were burned in the accident.
   Petra _____ *had her arms burned / burnt* _____ in the accident. **HAD**

8 They'll take your phone away if you use it while you're doing the test.
   Your _____ *phone will be taken* _____ away if you use it while you're doing the test. **BE**

21

Vocabulary

Collocations and expressions

8 Circle the correct option to complete the collocations and expressions.

1 *an abroad /* a foreign */ a travelling* language
2 *can't* help */ offer / give* doing something
3 *be keen at /* on */ for*
4 *dream for / with /* of *doing something*
5 *make /* give */ do encouragement*
6 *borrow / book /* browse *the internet*
7 *a* dream */ sleep / bed job*
8 *a virtual research /* tour */ information*

9 Complete the sentences with the correct form of the collocations and expressions from Exercise 8.

1 They spent a couple of hours ___*browsing the internet*___ for different craft workshops they could do.
2 My parents have always ___*dreamed / dreamt of doing*___ a road trip along the west coast of the USA.
3 If I could learn any ___*foreign language*___ I think I'd learn Japanese.
4 Children who are ___*given encouragement*___ are generally more confident than those who aren't.
5 He had had two bikes stolen, so he ___*wasn't keen on*___ buying a new one.
6 She signed up for a Spanish course that took her on a ___*virtual tour*___ of a different Spanish city each week.
7 When Penny didn't call, Seb ___*couldn't help*___ worrying.
8 Her ___*dream job*___ would be to work with children.

Exam practice

Open cloze

10 For each question, write the correct answer. Write one word for each gap.

1 She had a plant delivered to her mum ___*by*___ the local flower shop.
2 After getting a ___*degree*___ in biology at Durham University, she went to do research abroad.
3 He promised he ___*would*___ get the garage roof repaired before the winter.
4 I'm sorry, I think I've ___*made*___ a mistake.
5 He's from France and he speaks English with quite a strong French ___*accent*___ .
6 The school breaks ___*up*___ for the summer holidays next week.
7 There are three levels to choose from: beginner, ___*intermediate*___ and advanced.
8 Please fill in this application ___*form*___ if you're interested in the course.

Multiple-choice cloze

11 **For each question, choose the correct answer.**

1 My sister has her university ___ paid for by my parents.
 A applications B grants C fees D deposits

2 During the speaking test, the ___ showed us two photos and asked us to describe them.
 A examiner B instructor C coach D professor

3 He's a very clever pupil, but he doesn't ___ well in class, which gets him in trouble with the teacher.
 A pass B revise C behave D study

4 It isn't necessary to ___ notes during this lesson; I'll send the information to you by email.
 A do B create C take D read

5 If you want to stay in this club, you mustn't ___ any of the club rules.
 A give B make C smash D break

6 Students must hand in their research ___ by no later than 1st June.
 A certificates B diplomas C courses D projects

7 In my ___ class, we're learning about the value of different currencies.
 A economics B physics C IT D biology

8 He ___ marks in the exam because of his poor handwriting.
 A missed B lost C took D failed

Speaking

12 **Work in pairs. Discuss the questions.**

- What do you regularly have done for you?
- What have your parents had done to your house / flat in the last year?
- What will your school have had done by the end of the school year?
- What are you having done for you this week?
- What will you have had done by the end of the year?

Unit 22

Awareness

1 Which of these sentences are correct (C) and incorrect (I)?

1 Joe is very bad at play badminton.   I

2 They regret not moving to a different city when they went to university.   C

3 It isn't worth arguing with the teacher; she'll make you do the test again.   C

4 We arranged meeting our friends in a Brazilian restaurant.   I

5 They went to the lab to do an experiment.   C

6 I was sad hearing the news that you had failed the course.   I

7 He wasn't good enough to play in the team.   C

8 You should telling the coach if you're going to be late for training.   I

9 We'd prefer to take the bus than walk.   C

10 Mum and Dad persuaded me learning how to drive.   I

How many did you get right? ☐

Grammar

-ing form

We can use the *-ing* form:

- as a noun – either as the subject or object of a sentence.
Climbing is my favourite sport. *(subject)*
Tina likes *skateboarding*. *(object)*

- after prepositions.
*Kit is only four, but he's very good at **singing**.*

- after the verb *go* when we talk about activities.
*My family is going **skiing** at the weekend.*

We also use the *-ing* form after certain verbs and phrases.

admit	(don't) mind	have difficulty	like	risk
avoid	enjoy	imagine	love	spend
be used to	fancy	involve	miss	time
can't help	feel like	it's no good	practise	suggest
can't stand	finish	it's no use	prefer	
deny	forgive	it's (not) worth	prevent	
dislike	hate	keep	regret	

*Some students **have been spending time planning** the end-of-school party.*
*I **don't feel like revising** for my exam right now. I think I'll go for a walk.*

to + infinitive

We use *to* + infinitive:

- to explain purpose.
*He went to France **to learn** how to cook.*

- after adjectives such as *afraid, scared, happy, glad, sad.*
*She was **afraid to look down** in case she fell.*

- after *too* + adjective and adjective + *enough*.
*It's **too early to know** what he wants to do after he's finished college.*
*Their project wasn't **good enough to win** a prize.*

We also use *to* + infinitive after certain verbs and phrases.

afford	begin	hope	persuade	seem
agree	choose	invite	plan	start
allow	decide	learn	prepare	want
appear	expect	manage	pretend	would like
arrange	fail	need	promise	
ask	forget	offer	refuse	

Infinitives (without *to*)

We use infinitives (without *to*) after modal verbs.
You **should go** to the Careers Day to get some ideas about what you can do in the future.

-ing form or *to* + infinitive?

Some verbs can be followed by the *-ing* form or *to* + infinitive with no change in meaning. Some common verbs are *begin, bother, continue, hate, like, love* and *start*.
The students **began cleaning** / **to clean** the classroom at ten o'clock.
Joe knew he would fail the test, so he **didn't bother taking** / **to take** it.
Ms Marks **continued speaking** / **to speak** until the bell rang.
We **love hanging out** / **to hang out** with our friends.
Don't **start writing** / **to write** until I tell you to.

There are other verbs that can be followed by the *-ing* form or *to* + infinitive, but the meaning changes. Some common ones are *regret, forget, go on, remember, stop* and *try*.
I **regret telling** my secrets to Jane . *(I told my secrets to Jane, but now I wish I hadn't.)*
I **regret to tell** you that you have failed both of the exams. *(I am sorry that I have to give you this news.)*

Tim **forgot meeting** Iris at the party last year. *(He didn't remember that he had met her.)*
Tim **forgot to meet** his friends at the café. *(Tim didn't remember he had arranged to meet his friends at the café.)*

Mrs Smith **went on talking** about art for hours! *(She continued to talk about the same thing.)*
Mrs Smith **went on to talk** about art. *(She'd been talking about a different subject, and then started talking about a new subject – art.)*

My sister **remembered taking** a train with Grandma when she was four. *(She took a train when she was four and one day she remembered the event.)*
My sister **remembered to take** her project to school. *(She remembered first and then took her project to school.)*

I **stopped drinking** coffee in the evening. *(I used to drink coffee in the evening, but now I don't.)*
I **stopped to say** hi to Ali on the street. *(I stopped walking so I could start talking to Ali on the street.)*

If you want to get fitter, **try going** to the gym. *(You can go to the gym, but it might not help you.)*
If you travel to Italy, **try to go** to Verona. *(You might not be able to do it.)*

22

Grammar exercises

2 Choose the correct option to complete the sentences.

1 Jake's favourite sport is *swimming* / *to swim*.
2 You're good enough *play* / *to play* in the national team!
3 I would like *to know* / *knowing* why you haven't done your homework.
4 Come on. I don't mind *to drive* / *driving* you to band practice.
5 You should *switch* / *switching* your mobile off when you go to sleep.
6 If you don't mind, I think I want *being* / *to be* alone right now – I'm a bit upset.
7 I'm not very good at *play* / *playing* video games.
8 My friends and I are going *cycle* / *cycling* this evening.
9 We prefer *studying* / *study* in the school library.
10 Jack browsed the internet *looking* / *to look* up some information about film-making.

3 Match the beginnings of the sentences (1–8) with their endings (a–h).

1 I spend a lot of time   *e*   a living on her own. She's very lonely.
2 We've arranged   *c*   b be very proud of you for winning 1st prize!
3 Toby loves   *g*   c to meet Grandma and Grandad for a walk this afternoon.
4 Don't start   *d*   d running until I say 'go'.
5 She can't stand   *a*   e hanging out in the park with my friends.
6 It's no good   *h*   f to buy some milk on the way home.
7 They must   *b*   g playing badminton in his free time.
8 I forgot   *f*   h complaining about the weather – just take an umbrella with you!

4 Choose the correct option (a–c) to complete the sentences.

1 You should ___ a good night's sleep; you've got a big day tomorrow.
   a getting   (b) get   c to get

2 Your sister can't help ___ at you when you leave the bathroom in a mess.
   (a) yelling   b to yell   c yell

3 You can ___ the application form online.
   a to complete   b completing   (c) complete

4 She called ___ me what we had to do for homework.
   a asking   b ask   (c) to ask

5 Bram admitted ___ about his exam results.
   a to lie   b lie   (c) lying

6 Are you used to ___ in total darkness?
   a sleep   (b) sleeping   c to sleep

7 I was afraid ___ her for help, but now I'm glad I did.
   (a) to ask   b asking   c ask

8 The test seemed ___ easy, but the whole class ended up failing it.
   (a) to be   b being   c be

5 Complete the sentences with *to* + infinitive or the *-ing* form of the verbs.

1 Carlo will never forget _____*diving*_____ (dive) in the Great Barrier Reef.

2 I remember _____*eating*_____ (eat) homemade cakes in my grandmother's kitchen when I was a child.

3 The flowers were so pretty and colourful that we stopped _____*to take*_____ (take) photos of them.

4 First, the teacher talked about poetry, and then she went on _____*to discuss*_____ (discuss) novel writing.

5 The man at the cinema refused _____*to stop*_____ (stop) talking on his phone during the film!

6 We regret _____*to inform*_____ (inform) you that your train has been delayed.

7 Oh no! I forgot _____*to do*_____(do) my homework!

8 I regret _____*using*_____ (use) her camera without asking her first.

9 Patricia stopped _____*going*_____ (go) on holidays with her parents last year.

10 Luckily, Vince remembered _____*to buy*_____ (buy) his wife a gift for their wedding anniversary.

6 Complete the sentences about you. Use *to* + infinitive or the *-ing* form. *Students' own answers*

1 I'd prefer _____.

2 My friends and I dislike _____.

3 I sometimes go to the shops _____.

4 My classmates and I spend a lot of time _____.

5 I remember _____.

6 I'm too _____.

7 I often have difficulty _____.

8 I miss _____.

9 I can't afford _____.

10 My family may _____.

7 Complete the sentences with *to* + infinitive or the *-ing* form of the verbs.

1 You don't have to thank me; I was happy _____*to help*_____ .

2 Why do you keep _____*taking*_____ (take) my clothes without asking?

3 I can't believe it! I've been invited _____*to go*_____ (go) to Emilia's party.

4 It was a lot of hard work, but we finally managed _____*to finish*_____ (finish) the project.

5 Does your daughter plan _____*to travel*_____ (travel) when she leaves college?

6 Once your room is clean, you'll be allowed _____*to spend*_____ (spend) time with your friends.

7 I regret _____*to say*_____ (say) that your son's grades aren't good enough for the university _____*to accept*_____ (accept) him.

8 You should stop _____*complaining*_____ (complain) and just get on with your homework.

9 If you choose _____*to cycle*_____ (cycle) without a helmet, you risk _____*getting*_____ (get) injured.

10 Why are you pretending _____*to do*_____ (do) research? I know you turned the computer on _____*to surf*_____ (surf) the internet.

22

Vocabulary

Prepositions

8 Complete the sentences with these prepositions.

about (x2)	at (x2)	back	for	in	of	on	with

1 Maria found out _____*about*_____ her surprise party, but she pretended she didn't know.
2 You may be satisfied _____*with*_____ your results, but I think you can do better.
3 I asked my aunt what subjects she would choose if she went _____*back*_____ to school. She said literature and art.
4 Did you know that Pedro is thinking about applying _____*for*_____ a course at the college?
5 Tom left home _____*at*_____ eighteen and went to explore the world.
6 I hope to get a place _____*at*_____ a good university, but I need to get the grades.
7 If I need to concentrate _____*on*_____ something, I always listen to some classical music.
8 You should only eat a very small amount _____*of*_____ sugar – it's really bad for your health.
9 There has been an increase _____*in*_____ the number of students wanting to study technology.
10 Calm down, Megan. There's no use worrying _____*about*_____ something that may never happen!

Word formation

9 Use the word in capitals to form a word that fits in the gap.

1 Travelling is a great way to learn about different _____*cultures*_____ .   **CULTURAL**
2 What a delicious meal! I'm feeling very _____*satisfied*_____ .   **SATISFY**
3 All students are expected to follow the school _____*rules*_____ .   **RULER**
4 If you _____*revise*_____ every day, I'm sure you'll pass your test.   **REVISION**
5 Is Milo in primary or _____*secondary*_____ school this year?   **SECOND**
6 So many people have terrible _____*handwriting*_____ these days.   **HANDWRITTEN**
7 The new ski _____*instructor*_____ is very experienced.   **INSTRUCT**
8 Make sure you greet the _____*examiner*_____ politely when you enter the room.   **EXAM**

Exam practice

Open cloze

10 For each question, write the correct answer. Write one word for each gap.

1 My cousin is really bad _____*at*_____ paddleboarding – he keeps falling into the water.
2 The dancers weren't good _____*enough*_____ to win the talent show.
3 You must never _____*go*_____ climbing on your own – it's too dangerous.
4 I _____*would*_____ like to do a jewellery-making course in the future.
5 This appears _____*to*_____ be Joe's writing, but I can't be sure.
6 Today it's _____*too*_____ hot to go running.
7 If you don't answer all the questions on the exam paper, you _____*lose*_____ marks.
8 I can't believe I _____*passed*_____ my driving test! I'm so relieved I don't have to do it again.

Multiple-choice cloze

11 **For each question, choose the correct answer.**

1 James is learning Mandarin Chinese at the moment, and he's ___ good progress.
   A taking   B making   C doing   D having

2 We're providing food at the party, but if you want to bring ___ something else, you can.
   A forward   B through   C into   D along

3 The teacher gave me some really positive ___ on my project.
   A feedback   B effort   C research   D skill

4 I wish the instructor would stop yelling ___ me. It makes me very nervous!
   A to   B for   C in   D at

5 The long, dark winter months can leave people feeling quite lonely and ___ .
   A delighted   B curious   C depressed   D ashamed

6 The whole class got ___ marks on the test.
   A full   B complete   C total   D whole

7 I'm feeling good ___ our team today – I think they'll win!
   A around   B with   C about   D for

8 Juan's grammar and vocabulary are very good; he just needs to work more on his ___ .
   A animation   B pronunciation   C information   D explanation

Writing

12 **Read the writing task and write your answer in about 100–130 words. Try to use linking words and phrases.**

You receive a letter from your friend who tells you about a new course he / she is doing. Write a letter to your friend asking about the course and saying what kind of courses you would be interested in doing, and why.

Unit 23

Awareness

1 Which of these sentences are correct (C) and incorrect (I)?

1 Do you like my French cotton new scarf? ⊥

2 Tony is tired; he has been working in the lab all day. C

3 This course is bored; I wish I hadn't taken it. ⊥

4 We visit our grandparents regularly. C

5 Diana last week finished her degree in medicine. ⊥

6 Tess is quite good at solving puzzles. C

7 George isn't skilled enough to work as an architect. C

8 My mother's dream is to live in a nice little stone cottage by the sea. C

9 Dan placed gently the child on the bed after she had fallen asleep. ⊥

10 It was so a nice day that we decided to go swimming. ⊥

How many did you get right? ☐

Grammar

Gradable adjectives

Sometimes more than one adjective is used before a noun:
*He was a **shy young** man. She's got **long dark** hair.*

Some adjectives give a general opinion that we can use to describe almost any noun:
*He's a **good** doctor. It's a **bad** day. They're **lovely** friends.*

Other adjectives give a more specific opinion: they give us more information about the noun.
*a **delicious** pizza, a **friendly** girl*

Usually a general opinion adjective is placed before a specific opinion adjective:
*a **beautiful elegant** dress, a **cool trendy** restaurant*

When we use two or more adjectives to describe something / someone, we usually put them in this order.

Opinion	Size	Age	Shape	Colour	Origin	Material	
nice	small	old	round	pink	French	cotton	+ noun
beautiful	large	new	oval	blue	Italian	wooden	
strong	big	ancient	long	white	Japanese	silk	

*He has **nice short red** hair. Why does she wear that **horrible old orange** jacket?*

Adjectives ending in -ed and -ing

Adjectives that end in *-ed* describe how someone feels, whereas adjectives that end in *-ing* describe a person, place or thing.
*She's **interested** in the human body. She thinks working as a doctor would be very **interesting**.*

Types of adverbs

There are adverbs of frequency, manner, time, place and degree.

- Adverbs of frequency, answer the question *How often?*
*We go to see the dentist **regularly**.*

- Adverbs of manner answer the question *How?*
*She plays the piano **beautifully**.*

- Adverbs of time answer the question *When?*
*Sienna injured her ankle **last week**.*

- Adverbs of place answer the question *Where?*
*There is a medical centre **near my block of flats**.*

- Adverbs of degree answer the question *To what extent?*
*It's **rather** cold today; I think I'll wear my jacket.*

Order of adverbs (manner, place and time)

When we use two or more adverbs in a sentence, the usual order is manner + place + time.
*She put the letter **carefully into her bag after leaving the post office**.*

After verbs like *come, leave, go,* etc., the usual order is place + manner + time.
*He walked **to the hospital quickly after finishing his meeting**.*

Time adverbs can also come at the beginning of a sentence.
***After leaving the post office**, she put the letter carefully into her bag.*
***After finishing his meeting,** he walked quickly to the hospital.*

Order of adverbs (degree and frequency)

Adverbs of degree such as *quite, rather, too* and *very* usually come before an adjective.
*I am **quite** good at biology.*
*The book was **rather** silly.*

Enough is also an adverb of degree, but it comes after an adjective or a verb.
*The film wasn't **good enough** to win an award.*
*We **have enough** money to get two of these cakes.*

Adverbs of frequency such as *always, never, seldom,* etc. usually come after the verb *be,* but before the main verb.
*He **is always** home in the morning.*
*She **seldom eats** meat.*

so and such

We use *so* and *such* for emphasis. They are stronger than *very*.
- We use *so* + adjective / adverb.
*This film is **so exciting**! I'm really glad you suggested it!*
- We use *such* + (adjective) + noun.
*Your baby is **such** a beautiful child!*

We can also use *so* and *such* to emphasise characteristics that lead to a certain result or action.
*It was **such an exciting film that** I went to see it three times.*
*The meal was **so bad that** we left the restaurant without finishing it.*

Grammar exercises

2 Look at the list of adjectives and write opinion (OP), origin (OR), colour (C), size (S) or material (M).

1 English *OR*
2 French *OR*
3 glass *M*
4 gorgeous *OP*
5 horrible *OP*
6 huge *S*
7 Italian *OR*
8 lovely *OP*
9 metal *M*
10 purple *C*
11 red *C*
12 small *S*
13 tiny *S*
14 white *C*
15 leather *M*

3 Write the adjectives in order.

1 a(n) English / huge / stone / castle
   a huge English stone castle

2 a(n) wooden / antique / round / table
   an antique round wooden table

3 a colourful / cool / big / balloon
   a cool big colourful balloon

4 Italian / expensive / modern / sunglasses
   expensive modern Italian sunglasses

5 a(n) tall / glass / elegant / building
   an elegant tall glass building

6 a chocolate / small / tasty / dessert
   a tasty small chocolate dessert

7 a(n) comfortable / wool / orange / jumper
   a comfortable orange wool jumper

8 a(n) large / interesting / Mexican / bag
   an interesting large Mexican bag

23

4 Complete the sentences with the -ed or -ing form of the words.

1 I'm not saying the class was _____ *boring* _____ (bore), but the teacher spoke for too long.

2 Are you _____ *interested* _____ (interest) in the sciences, like biology and chemistry?

3 I am so _____ *bored* _____ (bore) right now – I've got nothing to do.

4 The brain is an _____ *amazing* _____ (amaze) thing.

5 We like all watersports, but they can be rather _____ *tiring* _____ (tire).

6 Sam said that she had read a very _____ *interesting* _____ (interest) article about neurons yesterday.

7 The children are _____ *exhausted* _____ (exhaust) after playing in the park all day.

8 Hans was really _____ *surprised* _____ (surprise) when he was told he had got the job.

5 Rewrite the sentences using the words. Sometimes more than one answer is possible.

1 Dad gets the car washed each month. (always)

Dad always gets the car washed each month.

Each month, Dad always gets the car washed.

2 I placed the glass bowl. (on the shelf / gently)

I placed the glass bowl gently on the shelf.

3 We bought some big straw hats. (rather / last year / at the beach)

We bought some rather big straw hats at the beach last year.

Last year at the beach, we bought some rather big straw hats.

4 Jackie has been listening to music. (all morning / happily)

Jackie has been happily listening to music all morning.

5 The doctor has been working. (all evening / at the hospital)

The doctor has been working at the hospital all evening.

6 She left. (noisily / the classroom / during the lesson)

She left the classroom noisily during the lesson.

During the lesson, she left the classroom noisily.

7 My sister cooks well. (usually / quite)

My sister usually cooks quite well.

8 They were feeling happy. (extremely / after the match)

They were feeling extremely happy after the match.

After the match, they were feeling extremely happy.

6 Complete the sentences with so, such, too or enough.

1 Billy is _____ *too* _____ young to know how to behave in restaurants.

2 It was _____ *such* _____ a scary film that many people left before it had finished.

3 My grades weren't good _____ *enough* _____ for me to get a place at university.

4 This book is _____ *so* _____ interesting! I can't put it down!

5 I think I've got just _____ *enough* _____ money to buy you a coffee and a piece of cake.

6 He's _____ *such* _____ a rude man. Why does he act like that?

7 The food was _____ *so* _____ bad that I refused to pay for it.

8 Are you tall _____ *enough* _____ to reach the top shelf, Jenna?

7 Choose the correct option (a–c) to complete the sentences.

1 I got a ___ scarf for my birthday.
   a silk beautiful Italian
   (b) beautiful Italian silk
   c beautiful silk Italian

2 You look ___ , Steven. Let's do something fun.
   (a) bored
   b bore
   c boring

3 Tony ___ ; I'm sure he'll win an award one day.
   a writes wonderful
   (b) writes wonderfully
   c wonderfully writes

4 Ben and Susana are ___ these days.
   a busy rather
   b rather busily
   (c) rather busy

5 I went ___ .
   (a) home quickly after school
   b home after school quickly
   c after school home quickly

6 His uncle is a ___ scientist.
   (a) very famous
   b very famously
   c famous very

7 He ___ to be able to bake a cake.
   a enough knows
   (b) knows enough
   c knowingly enough

8 It was ___ that I wanted to learn more.
   a too a fascinating subject
   b so a fascinating subject
   (c) such a fascinating subject

Vocabulary

Phrasal verbs

8 Complete the sentences with the correct form these phrasal verbs.

| back out of | fall off | go away | pick up | send back | shake off | think up | work out |

1 The little boy _____*fell off*_____ his bike and hurt his knees.
2 Can you help me _____*work out*_____ the answer to this puzzle, please?
3 You can't _____*back out of*_____ the appointment now. It's too late to cancel.
4 He's helping me _____*think up*_____ some new ways to get children interested in sport.
5 She went to the pharmacy to _____*pick up*_____ her tablets.
6 My parents _____*went away*_____ to the coast for a few days to celebrate their anniversary.
7 Your brain receives information from neurons in your skin, and then neurons in your brain _____*send*_____ a message _____*back*_____ to a part of your body to make it react.
8 Would you mind just _____*shaking off*_____ the leaves on the picnic blanket?

Word formation

9 Use the word in capitals to form a word that fits in the gap.

1 Jonas can't write with his right hand because he's _____*left-handed*_____ . **HAND**
2 Kay sews _____*incredibly*_____ well; you should get her to make your wedding dress. **INCREDIBLE**
3 Dad! Come _____*quickly*_____ . Our dog is chasing the neighbour's cat! **QUICK**
4 The woman had had a hard life, so she had many lines on her _____*forehead*_____ . **HEAD**
5 Don't worry – this is _____*easily*_____ fixed. **EASY**
6 I've got terrible _____*earache*_____ – it's so painful. **EAR**
7 Did you know that a person normally _____*breathes*_____ 23,000 times a day? **BREATH**
8 I read a book about the human body and I must say that I'm _____*amazed*_____ ! **AMAZE**

23

Exam practice

Open cloze

10 **For each question, write the correct answer. Write one word for each gap.**

1 The girl looked so hot that her mum took her _____ *temperature* _____ . It was forty degrees!
2 Please, can you stop the car? I _____ *feel* _____ really sick.
3 He broke his leg badly and went into hospital for an _____ *operation* _____ .
4 You should brush _____ *your* _____ teeth twice a day and avoid sugary snacks.
5 She's been unwell for a long time, but she's slowly recovering _____ *from* _____ the illness.
6 The elderly man wasn't breathing; they had to call an _____ *ambulance* _____ .
7 They wanted to lose weight, so they went _____ *on* _____ a diet.
8 I'm afraid you aren't _____ *making* _____ any sense. Tell me again, slowly, from the beginning.

Multiple-choice cloze

11 **For each question, choose the correct answer.**

1 Humans are the only animals that can bring their ___ all the way across to their little finger.
   (A) thumb   **B** hand   **C** heel   **D** chin

2 The man had a very long brown ___ .
   A hair   **(B)** beard   **C** teeth   **D** eyebrow

3 Parina fell and broke her ___ while she was playing football.
   A muscle   **B** lip   **C** stomach   **(D)** ankle

4 People who work at a desk all day often have problems with their ___ and back.
   A toes   **B** elbows   **(C)** shoulders   **D** knees

5 Why are you ___ your eye like that? Have you got something in it?
   A crying   **B** laughing   **(C)** blinking   **D** watering

6 It's impossible to keep your eyes open when you ___ .
   A breathe   **(B)** sneeze   **C** sleep   **D** cough

7 There's a man at the gym whose ___ are so large that he can only wear sleeveless T-shirts.
   A cells   **(B)** muscles   **C** bones   **D** lungs

8 Ouch! I was eating a biscuit and I bit my ___ .
   A tooth   **B** teeth   **C** throat   **(D)** tongue

Speaking

12 **Work in pairs. Discuss these things with your partner.**

- what his / her favourite item of clothing is like
- what the house / flat he / she lives in is like
- how well he / she can cook / sing /dance / do sport
- how often he / she goes to the dentist
- how healthy he / she thinks his / her life is

Awareness

1 **Which of these sentences are correct (C) and incorrect (I)?**

1 Have elephants got larger brains than humans? _C_
2 Jason has big feet than me. _I_
3 My father is intelligent than your father. _I_
4 Can your classmates run faster than you? _C_
5 A degree in medicine is one of the hardest to get. _C_

6 That was best course I've ever done. _I_
7 This is the tidiest I've ever seen your room! _C_
8 Tom reads good, but his writing needs some work. _I_
9 Swimming is my least favourite sport. _C_
10 He's not fit as his cousin. _I_

How many did you get right?

Grammar

Comparison of adjectives and adverbs

We use the comparative to compare two people or things. We usually form the comparative by adding *-er* to an adjective or adverb. If the adjective or adverb has two or more syllables, we use the word *more*. We often use the word *than* after the comparative.
*Beth has got **shorter** hair **than** Pam.*
*This silver smartphone is **more expensive than** the black one.*

We use the superlative to compare one person or thing with other people or things of the same type. We usually form the superlative by adding *-est* to the adjective or adverb. If the adjective or adverb has two or more syllables, we usually use the word *most*. We use *the* before the superlative.
*That was **the hardest** workout I've ever done.*
*She's **the most interesting** person we've ever met.*

Spelling: big → bi**gger** / bi**ggest**, nice → nic**er** / nic**est**, tidy → ti**dier** / ti**diest**

Some adjectives and adverbs are irregular.

Adjective / Adverb	Comparative	Superlative
good / well	better	the best
bad / badly	worse	the worst
many	more	the most
much	more	the most
little	less	the least
far	farther / further	the farthest / furthest

Other comparative structures

We use *as* + adjective / adverb + *as* to show that two people or things are similar in some way.
*My legs are **as long as** your legs.*

We use *not as / so ... as* to show that one person or thing has less of a quality than another.
*I am not **so big as** my brother.*

24

Grammar exercises

2 Complete the table.

Adjective / Adverb	Comparative	Superlative
bad / badly	1 _worse_	2 _the worst_
beautifully	3 _more beautifully_	4 _the most beautifully_
carefully	5 _more carefully_	6 _the most carefully_
exciting	7 _more exciting_	8 _the most exciting_
far	9 _farther / further_	10 _the farthest / the furthest_
late	11 _later_	12 _the latest_
little	13 _less_	14 _the least_
sad	15 _sadder_	16 _the saddest_
tasty	17 _tastier_	18 _the tastiest_
tidy	19 _tidier_	20 _the tidiest_

3 Complete the sentences with words from Exercise 2.

1 Why is your sister's room _____tidier_____ than yours? Yours is a complete mess!
2 Do you do _____less_____ exercise than your parents or more?
3 It's four in the morning! This is _____the latest_____ I've ever stayed up in my life!
4 Dad is ___the most careful___ driver I know. He has never had an accident.
5 My house is ___farther / further___ from the hospital than yours.
6 Weather forecasters say that this winter is going to be _____worse_____ than last winter.
7 That was _____the tastiest_____ curry I've ever eaten – you must give me the recipe.
8 If you asked me, I'd say that surfing is _____more exciting_____ than windsurfing. But I love doing both!
9 Look at these two paintings. Do you think Julia paints _____more beautifully_____ than her sister?
10 That was _____the saddest_____ story I've ever heard.

4 Choose the correct option to complete the sentences.

1 Karl runs *fastest* / *faster* than Dan – I think he'll win the race.
2 Dasha is rather unkind – she's *less* / *the least* popular girl in the school.
3 Which planet is *the furthest* / *further* from the sun?
4 Paul is *the younger* / *the youngest* doctor in the hospital.
5 Iraj is *more cleverer* / *more clever* than Steven.
6 This article about the brain is the *more interesting* / *the most interesting* I've read in a long time.
7 Fran is *good* / *better* at maths than me, but she's *worse* / *bad* at biology than me.
8 That is *the unhealthiest* / *the most unhealthiest* meal I've ever eaten.
9 I have *much* / *more* time to have fun in the summer than in the winter.
10 All the students in the class work hard, but George studies *the hardest* / *the harder*.

5 **Choose the correct option (a–c) to complete the sentences.**

1 This equipment is ___ than yours.
   a the heavier
   b the heaviest
   c⃝ heavier

2 Cara sang the ___ of all the children in the performance.
   a more happier
   b⃝ most happily
   c most happily than

3 This is ___ day we've had this summer – drink plenty of water!
   a⃝ the hottest
   b so hottest
   c the hotter

4 I am ___ you.
   a so fit as
   b⃝ as fit as
   c as fit so

5 This medicine is ___ that the one I usually buy.
   a the most expensive than
   b⃝ more expensive than
   c the more expensive than

6 They both work messily, but Clem works ___ than Joe.
   a⃝ more messily
   b most messily
   c the more messily

7 The medical centre is ___ from my house than the pharmacy.
   a the furthest
   b farthest
   c⃝ farther

8 They both have exams, but Luke isn't ___ his brother.
   a as stressed so
   b as stressed than
   c⃝ so stressed as

6 **Complete the sentences with your own opinions and the correct comparative or superlative form of the adjectives. Add words where necessary.** *Students' own answers but for the adjectives and example 1 as follows:*

1 When it comes to sports, I don't think _____*skiing*_____ is as _____*challenging*_____ (challenging) as ___*mountain climbing*___ .

2 So far, _____ is ___*the most beautiful*___ (beautiful) place I've ever visited.

3 I think that the _____ is _____*the scariest*_____ (scary) animal of all.

4 When comparing school subjects, I feel that _____ is _____*as difficult*_____ (difficult) as _____ .

5 _____ is _____*the friendliest*_____ (friendly) person I've ever met.

6 In my opinion, my _____ is _____*as good as*_____ (good) yours.

24

7 Complete the second sentence so that it has a similar meaning to the first sentence, using the word given. Do not change the word given. You must use between two and five words.

1 Jon is bigger than Greg.
Greg is not _____*so big as*_____ Jon. | **SO**

2 We've never performed such an extraordinary operation.
It's _____*the most*_____ extraordinary operation we've ever performed. | **THE**

3 All the doctors treat their patients well, but Doctor Collins treats his patients even better.
Doctor Collins __*treats his patients the best*__ of all the doctors. | **BEST**

4 Shuba is sicker than Tim.
Tim ____*isn't / is not as sick as*____ Shuba. | **AS**

5 My uncle is 35 years old and my aunt is 40 years old.
My aunt ____*is five years older than*____ my uncle. | **FIVE**

6 She is a hard worker who wants success. Her brother doesn't work hard enough.
She ____*works harder than*____ her brother to be successful. | **HARDER**

7 This glass is a quarter full of water. This bottle is half full of water. This vase is full of water.
The glass has got _____*the least*_____ water of all. | **THE**

8 Today's weather isn't as nice as yesterday's.
The weather today ____*is worse than it was*____ yesterday. | **WORSE**

Vocabulary

8 Complete the table.

Noun	Verb	Adjective	Adverb
automation	automate	automatic	1 ___*automatically*___
2 _*beauty*_ / beautician	beautify	beautiful	beautifully
energy	energise	3 ___*energetic*___	energetically
4 ___*injury*___	injure	injured / injuring	–
length	5 ___*lengthen*___	long / lengthy	–
6 ___*prescription*___	prescribe	prescriptive	prescriptively
sense	sense	7 _*sensory*_ / sensitive	sensorially /sensitively
8 ___*weight*___	weigh	weighty	–

9 Complete the sentences with words from Exercise 8.

1 My sister and I have both got red hair, but mine isn't as _____*long*_____ as hers.

2 The beating of our hearts is _____*automatic*_____ – we don't have to think about it.

3 The doctor should be able to _____*prescribe*_____ something to help with your earache.

4 The hairs on the back of your neck can stand up when you _____*sense*_____ danger.

5 The athlete has got an _____*injured*_____ foot at the moment and can't compete.

6 How much does her baby _____*weigh*_____ now? He's growing so fast!

7 After a tiring week at work, they didn't have any _____*energy*_____ to go out.

8 It was a great performance. He sang that slow song _____*beautifully*_____ .

Exam practice

Open cloze

10 **For each question, write the correct answer. Write one word for each gap.**

1 Some of the human body's largest _____*organs*_____ are the skin, the brain, the lungs and the heart.
2 He felt much better today _____*than*_____ yesterday.
3 For me, _____*the*_____ best thing about doing exercise is how good you feel after it.
4 After the night shift, all the doctors were as exhausted _____*as*_____ the nurses.
5 When you exercise, your heart _____*beats*_____ faster.
6 She cut her leg badly and lost quite a lot of _____*blood*_____ .
7 They put _____*on*_____ weight when they were on holiday in Italy.
8 She's sociable, but she's the _____*least*_____ sociable in her family.

Multiple-choice cloze

11 **For each question, choose the correct answer.**

1 Is your house ___ away from the gym than mine?
   A farthest   **B** far   **C** farther   **D** furthest

2 He's got ___ money than you – you should pay for the meal!
   A little   **B** least   **C** less   **D** fewer

3 Kurt is a really ___ person to hang out with; you never know what fun thing he'll do next.
   A curious   **B** interested   **C** gorgeous   **D** exciting

4 She's got a terrible cough, which has given her a sore ___ .
   A throat   **B** chin   **C** shoulder   **D** neck

5 This is the ___ advanced lab equipment in the world.
   A enough   **B** most   **C** so   **D** too

6 Jake is more ___ about failing his physics exam than Pavel, who isn't worried at all.
   A uncomfortable   **B** anxious   **C** tired   **D** bored

7 Why was Janek in such a bad ___ yesterday?
   A energy   **B** sense   **C** feeling   **D** mood

8 In class, Oliver chats more ___ with the other children than Arif.
   A easily   **B** easy   **C** easiest   **D** ease

Writing

12 **Read the writing task and write your answer in about 100–130 words. Try to use formal language.**

Write an essay answering this question:
How can schools help students have a healthier lifestyle? Give some examples from your own experience.

Grammar

1 **Rewrite the sentences with the causative.**

1   Someone had installed new windows in their flat.
    They had / got new windows installed in their / the flat.

2   Ms Scott must make the team's uniforms by the end of the month.
    The team must have / get their uniforms made by Ms Scott by the end of the month.

3   A carpenter is going to make a chest of drawers for me.
    I'm going to have / get a chest of drawers made (for me) by a carpenter.

4   Lia's uncle will fix her shower for her.
    Lia will have / get her shower fixed (for her) by her uncle.

5   New computers were delivered to Dad's office.
    Dad's office had / got new computers delivered.

6   Billy's skateboard was stolen at the park.
    Billy had his skateboard stolen at the park.

7   Are they planting a garden inside the school?
    Are they having / getting a garden planted inside the school?

8   Someone walks the Smiths' dog every day.
    The Smiths have / get their dog walked every day.

2 **Complete the sentences with the infinitive or the *-ing* form of the verbs.**

1   Teachers expect students *to hand in* (hand in) their essays on time.
2   Would you enjoy *going* (go) on a course where you could learn about nature?
3   You could *become* (become) healthier by eating properly and doing lots of exercise.
4   How much time do most students spend *surfing* (surf) the internet each week?
5   Jamal, would you like *to come* (come) to the end-of-term party with us?
6   They must *try* (try) harder than that if they want to get good grades.
7   We can use photographic satellites *to help* (help) understand our world.
8   Young children learn how to behave by *following* (follow) the examples of others.
9   Here, we aim to *to educate* (educate) children so they become responsible and kind adults.
10 He told the class about the importance of *drinking* (drink) water regularly.

3 **Choose the correct option (a–b) to complete the sentences.**

1   That was an ___ video; play it again!
    a amazing
    b amazed

2   It was ___ that I wanted to stay there for longer.
    a such a nice island
    b so a nice island

3   Doesn't Ms Jackson ___ ? I love her voice.
    a beautifully sing
    b sing beautifully

4   The teacher walked ___ .
    a home quickly after classes were over
    b after classes were over home quickly

5   It's ___ today.
    a rather warm
    b rather warmly

6   There were ___ flowers around the door.
    a colourful big lovely
    b lovely big colourful

7   Professor Harper is a ___ speaker and writer.
    a very cleverly
    b very clever

8   Ahmed is ___ to get that from the cupboard.
    a enough tall
    b tall enough

4 Complete the sentences with the comparative or superlative form of the words. Add words where necessary.

1 He's got _____ more _____ (many) books than anyone else I know.

2 Ms Patten marks our work _____ more carefully _____ (carefully) than Mr Jones, but they're both good teachers.

3 My sister gets good grades _____ more easily _____ (easily) than I do.

4 You're _____ the best _____ (good) cook I know; could you make dinner tonight?

5 Mum got me a new wardrobe for my birthday; it was _____ the biggest _____ (big) one in the shop.

6 Is the secondary school _____ farther / further _____ (far) away from Elm Street than the primary school?

7 Biology is _____ the most interesting _____ (interesting) subject at school. I love learning about the human body.

8 These builders work _____ the most tidily _____ (tidily) of all the builders I've employed – they clear up the mess they make every day.

5 Tick the correct sentences. Then correct the mistakes.

1 Do you think that your schedule is as busier as mine?
   Do you think that your schedule is busier than / as busy as mine?

2 My boyfriend drives a big old white van.
   ✓

3 In my opinion, last year's holiday wasn't so relaxing so this year's.
   In my opinion, last year's holiday wasn't so relaxing as this year's.

4 My grandfather can't hear as good as my grandmother, but he can see better than her.
   My grandfather can't hear as well as my grandmother, but he can see better than her.

5 I'm afraid the head teacher is too busy speaking with you right now.
   I'm afraid the head teacher is too busy to speak with you right now.

6 The children stopped seeing the little bird sitting by the window.
   The children stopped to see the little bird sitting by the window.

7 My brother is interested in to become a journalist.
   My brother is interested in becoming a journalist.

8 They usually meet after class regularly for a coffee.
   They usually meet regularly after class for a coffee.

9 My mum is going to cut her hair tomorrow by a famous hairdresser.
   My mum is going to have / get her hair cut tomorrow by a famous hairdresser.

10 Will that artist have his sculptures exhibited at the gallery next month?
   ✓

6 Choose the correct option to complete the sentences.

1 This is a very *depressed* / *depressing* documentary; I think I'll go to bed.
2 Looking after your body is *such* / *so* important.
3 It was *such* / *very* a gorgeous day that I decided to take some time off work.
4 Stuart *will check his eyes* / *will have his eyes* checked at the hospital today.
5 We're having some trees planted *for* / *by* professionals.
6 Oh no! I forgot *to bring* / *bringing* my maths book home from school!
7 Students must *to hand in* / *hand in* their projects by tomorrow.
8 We went to the gym *to lift* / *lifting* some weights.
9 The baby wakes up *earlier* / *the earliest* than the rest of the children.
10 Harry speaks *the most quietly* / *the more quiet* of all the boys in the class.

Use of English

Open cloze

7 For each question, write the correct answer. Write one word for each gap.

1 I was very glad _____*to*_____ hear that you got into university.
2 They've backed _____*out*_____ of the holiday plan as they can't afford it.
3 Nina _____*had*_____ her arm broken when a cyclist rode into her.
4 We're having the laptop repaired _____*by*_____ a computer company.
5 Could you concentrate _____*on*_____ doing your homework, please?
6 _____*Have*_____ they had a new front door made for their house?
7 My brother complains _____*more*_____ than other brothers – I'm sure of it!
8 I know you can do it. You're _____*making*_____ really good progress.
9 That was _____*the*_____ most difficult exam I've ever taken.
10 Jo can write stories _____*as*_____ well as her sister Kate.

Word formation

8 Use the word in capitals to form a word that fits in the gap.

1 It's amazing how _____*energetic*_____ children are, even after a day at school! **ENERGY**
2 Just because she's got all her qualifications, it doesn't mean she will _____*automatically*_____ get a job. **AUTOMATE**
3 I strongly believe the expression ' _____*beauty*_____ is on the inside'. **BEAUTIFUL**
4 Grandad has been _____*prescribed*_____ some new tablets by his doctor. **PRESCRIPTION**
5 They want to lose a bit of _____*weight*_____ , so they've started eating more healthily. **WEIGH**
6 Can you name your _____*sensory*_____ organs? **SENSE**
7 He needs to use a walking stick due to an old _____*injury*_____ . **INJURE**
8 They had to _____*lengthen*_____ her stay in hospital because she wasn't getting better. **LONG**

Grammar

9 For questions 1–10, choose the word or phrase that best completes the sentence.

1 Is Joel ___ to join the swimming team?
A very good
(B) good enough
C so good
D the better

2 ___ by a babysitter in the evening?
A Do her children look after
B Does she look after her children
C Are her children look after
(D) Does she have her children looked after

3 The candidates ___ by the manager.
A will get their job application review
B will review their job application
(C) will have their job application reviewed
D will have reviewed their job application

4 ___ is the best sport in the world.
A Ski
B To ski
(C) Skiing
D The skiing

5 George ___ at the gym today.
A is having his phone stolen
(B) had his phone stolen
C had stolen his phone
D had been stealing his phone

6 Liz ___ ; it's part of her job.
(A) always goes to the lab on Monday
B goes always to the lab on Monday
C on Monday goes always to the lab
D goes to always the lab on Monday

7 It's getting cold outside; you should ___ a jumper.
A to wear
(B) wear
C wearing
D be wear

8 Feta is a ___ cheese that is delicious in salads.
A white nice tasty Greek
B nice Greek tasty white
C tasty white Greek nice
(D) nice tasty white Greek

9 I can't afford ___ you anywhere expensive.
(A) to take
B take
C taking
D for take

10 That was ___ soup I've ever had!
A worst
B much worse
(C) the worst
D as bad

Vocabulary

10 For questions 11–20, choose the word or phrase that best completes the sentence.

11 All the children received a ___ and a medal.
A degree
B project
C diploma
(D) certificate

12 I can't work ___ where the new lab is.
(A) out
B for
C on
D with

13 She isn't very ___ with her grades.
A interested
B excited
(C) satisfied
D annoyed

14 I bought some trousers online, but they were too tight, so I sent them ___ .
(A) back
B through
C on
D out

15 Let's give the players some more ___ .
A improvement
(B) encouragement
C appointment
D excitement

16 They want to ___ out about IT courses.
A discover
B look
C explore
(D) find

17 He's not too ___ on learning languages.
A glad
B proud
(C) keen
D curious

18 She can't ___ sneezing if she smells a flower.
A offer
(B) help
C try
D do

19 There's no use worrying ___ what may happen.
A around
(B) about
C of
D for

20 There's been a large ___ in car accidents.
(A) increase
B amount
C raise
D advance

Irregular verbs

Infinitive	Past simple	Past participle
be	was / were	been
beat	beat	beaten
become	became	become
begin	began	begun
bite	bit	bitten
blow	blew	blown
break	broke	broken
bring	brought	brought
broadcast	broadcast	broadcast
build	built	built
burn	burned / burnt	burned / burnt
buy	bought	bought
can	could	–
catch	caught	caught
choose	chose	chosen
come	came	come
cost	cost	cost
cut	cut	cut
deal	dealt	dealt
dig	dug	dug
do	did	done
draw	drew	drawn
dream	dreamed / dreamt	dreamed / dreamt
drink	drank	drunk
drive	drove	driven
eat	ate	eaten
fall	fell	fallen
feed	fed	fed
feel	felt	felt
fight	fought	fought
find	found	found
fly	flew	flown
forecast	forecast	forecast
forget	forgot	forgotten
get	got	got
give	gave	given
go	went	gone
grow	grew	grown
have	had	had
hear	heard	heard
hide	hid	hidden
hit	hit	hit
hold	held	held
hurt	hurt	hurt
keep	kept	kept
know	knew	known
lead	led	led
learn	learned / learnt	learned / learnt
leave	left	left
lend	lent	lent
let	let	let
lie	lay	lain

Infinitive	Past simple	Past participle
light	lit	lit
lose	lost	lost
mean	meant	meant
make	made	made
meet	met	met
pay	paid	paid
prove	proved	proven
put	put	put
read	read (pronounced /red/)	read (pronounced /red/)
ride	rode	ridden
ring	rang	rung
rise	rose	risen
run	ran	run
say	said	said
see	saw	seen
sell	sold	sold
send	sent	sent
set	set	set
shake	shook	shaken
shine	shone	shone
show	showed	shown
shoot	shot	shot
shut	shut	shut
sing	sang	sung
sink	sank	sunk
sit	sat	sat
sleep	slept	slept
slide	slid	slid
smell	smelled / smelt	smelled / smelt
speak	spoke	spoken
spend	spent	spent
stand	stood	stood
steal	stole	stolen
stick	stuck	stuck
stink	stank	stunk
swim	swam	swum
take	took	taken
teach	taught	taught
tell	told	told
think	thought	thought
throw	threw	thrown
understand	understood	understood
wake	woke	woken
wear	wore	worn
win	won	won
write	wrote	written

Phrasal verbs

back out of	=	decide not to do something you said you would do	(U23)
be into	=	very interested and involved in something	(U19)
break into	=	force your way into something or somewhere	(U21)
break up	=	when classes stop and holidays start	(U21)
bring along	=	take something or someone with you	(U22)
bring up	=	care for a child until it is an adult	(U2)
carry on	=	continue	(U12)
carry out	=	do or complete something	(U18)
check out	=	leave a hotel room after paying	(U13)
cheer on	=	encourage someone loudly	(U11)
clean up	=	make a place clean and tidy	(U6)
come back	=	return to a place	(U13)
come out (of)	=	appear from	(U3)
come round	=	go to someone's house	(U16)
cut up	=	cut into smaller pieces	(U3)
dream of	=	think about something you want	(U21)
eat out	=	eat in a restaurant	(U3)
end up	=	reach a place or be in a situation	(U19)
fall down	=	fall to the ground	(U9)
fall off	=	to separate from and move towards the ground	(U23)
fall over	=	fall to the ground	(U11)
fill in	=	complete	(U19)
find out	=	discover	(U3/18)
get along (with)	=	be friendly with	(U16)
get on (with someone)	=	be friendly with	(U9)
get on (with something)	=	start or continue doing something	(U19)
get to	=	arrive at	(U3)
get together	=	meet in order to spend time together	(U16)
give up	=	stop doing something	(U16)
go away	=	leave home in order to spend time somewhere else	(U23)
go back	=	return	(U22)
go down (as)	=	be remembered as	(U11)
go on	=	continue	(U22)
go out	=	leave to do something for entertainment	(U3)
go out (with)	=	have a romantic relationship	(U2)
go with	=	look good together	(U8)
grow up	=	become an adult	(U9)
hand in	=	give something to a person of authority	(U16)
hang out (with)	=	spend time with friends	(U16)
join in	=	become part of a group activity	(U16)
kick off	=	start	(U11)

live without	=	survive	(U7)
look at	=	examine	(U8)
look out for	=	try to notice someone or something	(U3)
look up	=	get information about	(U3)
meet up	=	see and talk to someone after planning to do so	(U11)
move in	=	go to a different place and live there	(U13)
pay for	=	use money to buy something	(U8)
pick up	=	use your hands to take and hold something	(U8)
pick up	=	collect	(U23)
put away	=	put something in a place where it is usually kept	(U9)
put off	=	decide or arrange to delay an event or activity until later	(U19)
put on	=	organise an event	(U15)
put out	=	extinguish	(U2)
run out	=	leave somewhere while running	(U2)
run out (of something)	=	use something completely so that there is none left	(U6)
send back	=	return something	(U23)
set up	=	establish	(U10)
shake off	=	move up and down quickly to get rid of something	(U23)
shop around	=	look at the prices of a product in different shops before you buy	(U8)
show around	=	lead someone through a place	(U11)
sign up	=	agree to become involved in an organised group or activity	(U17)
split up	=	separate	(U2)
switch off	=	finish something by moving a switch of button	(U16)
take out	=	remove	(U3)
take up	=	begin a new activity	(U16)
tidy up	=	arrange something in a neat way	(U10)
think up	=	produce a new idea or plan	(U22)
try on	=	wear clothes to see if they fit and look good	(U8)
try out	=	test to see what something is like or if it is useful	(U11)
turn down	=	make something quieter	(U19)
turn into	=	change into someone or something different	(U19)
turn off	=	finish something by moving a switch of button	(U19)
turn on	=	start something by moving a switch or button	(U19)
turn out	=	end in a certain way	(U19)
turn up	=	make something louder	(U19)
warm up	=	prepare your body for exercise	(U11)
wear out	=	make something old so it can't be used anymore	(U8)
work out	=	solve	(U23)

Prepositions

an amount **of** something	(U22)
an increase **in** something	(U22)
appear **in**	(U5)
apply **for** something	(U1)
at (eighteen)	(U22)
at the end **of**	(U9)
at the moment	(U5)
be a long way **from** somewhere / someone	(U14)
be an expert **in** something	(U17)
be brought up **by** someone	(U2)
be close **to** somewhere	(U9)
be in trouble **with** someone	(U2)
be satisfied **with** something	(U22)
before it's too late	(U5)
book accommodation **for** something	(U14)
chat **with** someone	(U17)
click **on** something	(U17)
communicate **with** someone / something	(U17)
concentrate **on** something	(U22)
due **to** something	(U2)
(everything) **from** ... **to** ...	(U5/U19)
fight **for** something	(U2)
find out **about** something	(U22)
for (ten) years	(U5)
get a place **at** (university)	(U22)
get married **in**	(U2)
get on **with** someone	(U9)
get something **from**	(U9)
go back **to** school	(U19)
go **on** a boat trip	(U14)
go **on** foot	(U14)
go out **with** someone	(U2)
have a negative effect **on** something	(U14)
have access **to** something	(U17)
have permission **to** do something	(U14)
in the middle of	(U5)
in the past / future	(U9)
keep in touch **with** someone	(U17)
live **on** (the second floor)	(U9)
live **on** your own	(U9)
look **for** something / someone	(U17)
move **to** somewhere	(U9)
run out **into** something	(U2)
sign up **for** something	(U17)
spend money **on** something / someone	(U14)
split up **with** someone	(U2)
stay **at** home	(U14)
stay **for** (a week)	(U9)
succeed **in** something	(U17)
take someone **to** somewhere	(U5)
tell someone **about** something	(U14)
throw something **onto**	(U5)
travel **by** air	(U14)
turn something **into**	(U5)
upload something **to** somewhere	(U17)
wait a long time **for** something	(U2)
work **with** someone	(U2)
worry **about** something	(U22)
wrap (a blanket) **around** someone	(U9)

Collocations and expressions

a dream job	(U21)		go on a day trip	(U13)
a foreign language	(U21)		go to university	(U1)
a virtual tour	(U21)		have a good time	(U13)
add to your carbon footprint	(U13)		help someone with their homework	(U10)
apply for a job	(U1)		keep track of	(U18)
be a waste of time	(U18)		land a plane	(U6)
be easy to use	(U18)		make a hotel reservation	(U13)
be good value	(U18)		make a video call	(U18)
be half price	(U10)		make a video	(U1)
be keen on	(U21)		make your bed	(U10)
be yourself	(U18)		organise local events	(U6)
browse the internet	(U21)		prepare for a journey	(U13)
call the police	(U10)		recycle plastic	(U6)
can't help doing something	(U21)		reduce your use of electricity	(U6)
carry out (someone's) instructions	(U18)		send signals to	(U18)
change your mind	(U13)		start your own company	(U10)
clean up a park	(U6)		suffer from over-tourism	(U13)
collect data	(U18)		take a break	(U10)
design buildings	(U1)		take a seat	(U10)
dream of doing something	(U21)		take public transport	(U6)
get a job offer	(U10)		take time off	(U13)
get access to	(U10)		talk to your friends and family	(U6)
get annoyed with someone	(U1)		tidy up the garden	(U10)
get married	(U1)		travel into space	(U1)
give (someone) advice	(U1)		wait a long time	(U1)
give encouragement	(U21)		work on a project	(U1)
give personal information	(U18)		write a blog	(U6)

Word formation

Adjective → adjective

SECOND	SECONDARY	U22
SOCIAL	SOCIABLE	U1

Adjective → noun

ACTIVE	ACTING / ACTOR	U20
ATHLETIC	ATHLETICS / ATHLETE	U12
BEAUTIFUL	BEAUTY / BEAUTICIAN	U24
CHALLENGED / CHALLENGING	CHALLENGE	U12
CULTURAL	CULTURES	U22
CUSTOMARY	CUSTOM / CUSTOMER	U4
DIVING	DIVING / DIVER	U12
DRAMATIC	DRAMA	U20
ELECTRIC	ELECTRICITY	U5
EQUIPPED	EQUIPMENT	U20
FRESH	FRESHNESS	U4
HANDWRITTEN	HANDWRITING	U22
INJURED / INJURING	INJURY	U24
MUSICAL	MUSICIAN / MUSICAL	U20
PRESCRIPTIVE	PRESCRIPTION	U24
THRILLING / THRILLED	THRILL / THRILLER	U20
WEIGHTY	WEIGHT	U24

Adjective → verb

COMFORTABLE / UNCOMFORTABLE	COMFORT	U4
COMPETITIVE	COMPETE	U12
DANGEROUS / ENDANGERED / ENDANGERING	ENDANGER	U12
ENTERTAINING / ENTERTAINED	ENTERTAIN	U20
IMPROVED / IMPROVING	IMPROVE	U12
LONG / LENGTHY	LENGTHEN	U24
PERFORMING	PERFORM	U20
SUSTAINABLE	SUSTAIN	U4

Adverbs

ABSOLUTE	ABSOLUTELY	U3
ACTING / ACTOR	ACTIVELY	U15
ATHLETICS / ATHLETE	ATHLETICALLY	U12
AUTOMATION / AUTOMATE / AUTOMATIC	AUTOMATICALLY	U24
BEAUTY / BEAUTICIAN	BEAUTIFULLY	U24
CHALLENGE	CHALLENGINGLY	U12
COMPETE	COMPETITIVELY	U12
COORDINATED	COORDINATELY	U12
DEEP	DEEPLY	U12
DRAMA	DRAMATICALLY	U20
EASY	EASILY	U23
ENDANGER	DANGEROUSLY	U12
ENERGETIC	ENERGETICALLY	U24
ENTERTAIN	ENTERTAININGLY	U20
FREEDOM / FREE	FREELY	U12
IMPROVE	IMPROVINGLY / IMPROVABLY	U12
INCREDIBLE	INCREDIBLY	U23
INJURY	INJURIOUSLY	U24
MUSIC / MUSICIAN / MUSICAL	MUSICALLY	U20
PRESCRIPTION	PRESCRIPTIVELY	U24
QUICK	QUICKLY	U23
SENSORY	SENSORIALLY / SENSITIVELY	U24
STRONG	STRONGLY	U12
THRILL / THRILLER	THRILLINGLY	U20

Noun → adjective		
AWE	AWESOME	U15
BOREDOM	BORING / BORED	U4
BRIGHTNESS	BRIGHT	U4
CHEER	CHEERFUL	U1
COLOUR	COLOURFUL	U3
COORDINATION / COORDINATOR	COORDINATED / COORDINATING	U12
CREATIVITY	CREATIVE	U4
DEPTH	DEEP	U12
DISAPPOINTMENT	DISAPPOINTED	U7
ELEGANCE	ELEGANT	U7
ENERGY	ENERGETIC	U24
ENJOYMENT	ENJOYABLE	U15
EXPENSIVE	INEXPENSIVE	U3
FRIEND	FRIENDLY / UNFRIENDLY	U4
HAND	LEFT-HANDED	U23
IMPRESSION	IMPRESSED	U7
LOCALITY	LOCAL	U4
MISERY	MISERABLE	U1
MODERNISATION	MODERN	U20
MUSIC / MUSICIAN / MUSICAL	MUSICAL	U20
ORIGIN	ORIGINAL	U7
PROFESSION	PROFESSIONAL	U7
SENSE	SENSORY / SENSITIVE	U24
SPICE	SPICY	U3
STRENGTH	STRONG	U12
TERROR	TERRIBLE	U15
TREND	TRENDY	U4
VISION	VISIBLE	U5
WARMTH	WARMER	U5

Noun → Noun		
ACTING	ACTOR	U20
ATHLETICS	ATHLETE	U12
BEAUTY	BEAUTICIAN	U24
COMPETITION	COMPETITOR	U12
COORDINATION	COORDINATOR	U12
DIVING	DIVER	U12
EAR	EARACHE	U23
EXAM	EXAMINER	U22
HEAD	FOREHEAD	U23
LAW	LAWYER	U1
LIBRARY	LIBRARIAN	U1
MUSIC / MUSICAL	MUSICIAN	U20
OPERATION	OPERATOR	U1
PERFORMANCE	PERFORMER	U20
PHOTOGRAPH	PHOTOGRAPHY	U15
POLITICS	POLITICIAN	U1
RULER	RULES	U22

Noun → verb		
BREATH	BREATHE	U23
COMFORT	COMFORT	U4
COMPETITION / COMPETITOR	COMPETE	U12
DANGER	ENDANGER	U12
ENTERTAINMENT / ENTERTAINER	ENTERTAIN	U20
EXPRESSION	EXPRESS	U7
IMPROVEMENT	IMPROVE	U12
LENGTH	LENGTHEN	U24
PERFORMANCE / PERFORMER	PERFORM	U20
REVISION	REVISE	U22
SURVIVAL	SURVIVE	U5
SUSTAINABILITY	SUSTAIN	U4

Word formation

Verb → adjective		
ADVERTISE	ADVERTISING	U7
AMAZE	AMAZED	U23
AMAZE	AMAZING	U15
BEFRIEND	FRIENDLY / UNFRIENDLY	U4
BIODEGRADE	BIODEGRADABLE	U5
BORE	BORING / BORED	U4
BRIGHTEN	BRIGHT	U4
CONFUSE	CONFUSED	U7
CREATE	CREATIVE	U4
COORDINATE	COORDINATED / COORDINATING	U12
DEEPEN	DEEP	U12
EMPLOY	UNEMPLOYED	U1
ENERGISE	ENERGETIC	U24
FRIGHTEN	FRIGHTENING	U15
LOCALISE	LOCAL	U4
MODERNISE	MODERN	U20
PLEASE	PLEASANT	U15
PROCESS	PROCESSED	U3
RECYCLE	RECYCLING	U5
RELAX	RELAXED	U3
RELY	RELIABLE	U1
RENEW	RENEWABLE	U5
SATISFY	SATISFIED	U22
SCARE	SCARY	U15
SENSE	SENSORY / SENSITIVE	U24
SPARKLE	SPARKLING	U3
STRENGTHEN	STRONG	U12
TASTE	TASTELESS	U3
TREND	TRENDY	U4

Verb → noun		
ACT	ACTING / ACTOR	U20
BEAUTIFY	BEAUTY / BEAUTICIAN	U24
CHALLENGE	CHALLENGE	U12
CUSTOMISE	CUSTOM / CUSTOMER	U4
DIVE	DIVING / DIVER	U12
DRAMATISE	DRAMA	U20
EQUIP	EQUIPMENT	U20
EXAMINE	EXAMINER	U22
FRESHEN	FRESHNESS	U4
INJURE	INJURY	U24
INSTRUCT	INSTRUCTOR	U22
INVENT	INVENTOR	U5
PACK	PACKETS	U3
PRESCRIBE	PRESCRIPTION	U24
QUALIFY	QUALIFICATIONS	U1
RECOMMEND	RECOMMENDATIONS	U3
THRILL	THRILL / THRILLER	U20
WEIGH	WEIGHT	U24

Prefixes		
COMFORTABLE	UNCOMFORTABLE	U4
DANGEROUS	ENDANGERED / ENDANGERING	U12
EMPLOY	UNEMPLOYED	U1
EXPENSIVE	INEXPENSIVE	U3
FRIENDLY	UNFRIENDLY	U4
HAND	LEFT-HANDED	U23

National Geographic Learning,
a Cengage Company

***New Close-up English in Use B1 Teacher's Book,
Second Edition***
Author: Philip James

Additional material: Emma Fox

Program Director: Sharon Jervis

Editorial Manager: Claire Merchant

Project Manager: Adele Moss

Head of Strategic Marketing: Charlotte Ellis

Head of Production and Design: Celia Jones

Content Project Manager: Nick Lowe

Manufacturing Manager: Eyvett Davis

Cover Design: Geoff Ward

Compositors: Jonathan Bargus & Elisabeth Heissler
  Graphic Design

For permission to use material from this text or product,
submit all requests online at **cengage.com/permissions**
Further permissions questions can be emailed to
permissionrequest@cengage.com

Teacher's Edition:
ISBN: 978-1-473-78641-7

National Geographic Learning
Cheriton House, North Way,
Andover, Hampshire, SP10 5BE
United Kingdom

Locate your local office at **international.cengage.com/region**

Visit National Geographic Learning online at **ELTNGL.com**
Visit our corporate website at **www.cengage.com**

CREDITS

Photos: 9 © Sam Edwards/OJO Images/Getty Images; **12** © Antonio_Diaz/iStockphoto; **16** © Emely/Image Source/Getty Images; **20** © aluxum/E+/Getty Images; **21** © kupicoo/E+/Getty Images; **29** © Jeff Hunter/Photographer's Choice RF/Getty Images; **35** © Teresa Kopec/Moment/Getty Images; **40** © F.J. Jimenez/Moment/Getty Images; **44** © Justin Lambert/DigitalVision/Getty Images; **45** © SDI Productions/E+/Getty Images; **53** © Westend61/Getty Images; **54** © Westend61/Getty Images; **62** © Westend61/Getty Images; **63** Ziga Plahutar/E+/Getty Images; **65** © Lorado/E+/Getty Images; **69** © Paul Chesley/National Geographic Image Collection; **70** © Josep Suria/Shutterstock; **71** © Cavan Images/Cavan/Getty Images; 75 © kali9/E+/Getty Images; **83** © Oleg Breslavtsev/Moment/Getty Images; **85** © Monkey Business Images/Shutterstock; **86(t)** © zeljkosantrac/E+/Getty Images; **86(b)** © Daniel Milchev/DigitalVision/Getty Images; **88** © Imgorthand/E+/Getty Images; **92** © Dougal Waters/DigitalVision/Getty Images; **93** © ESB Professional/Shutterstock; **97** © Christopher Hopefitch/The Image Bank/Getty Images; **98** © Atlantide Phototravel/The Image Bank Unreleased/Getty Images; **102** © Rob Lewine/Getty Images; **108** © MARK GARLICK/Science Photo Library/Getty Images; **111** © Paper Boat Creative/DigitalVision/Getty Images; **113** © HEX/Getty Images; **116** SolStock/E+/Getty Images; **122** © Jena Ardell/Moment/Getty Images; **124** © Yuri_Arcurs/E+/Getty Images; **133** © MorphoBio/Shutterstock; **137** © Moyo Studio/E+/Getty Images; **138** © Cavan Images/Cavan/Getty Images; **139** © Ariel Skelley/DigitalVision/Getty Images; **143** © skynesher/E+/Getty Images; **148** © FatCamera/E+/Getty Images; **149** © Image Source/Getty Images; **151** © Mara Brandl/Getty Images

ON THE COVER

The cover image shows the inside of the Jin Mao Tower in Shanghai, China. The skyscraper is 420.5 metres (1,380 feet) tall and contains offices, a 5-star hotel and an observation deck. In the basement there is parking for 2,000 bicycles!
© Matthias Lenke/Okapia/Robert Harding

Printed in Greece by Bakis, SA
Print Number: 01   Print Year: 2022